Spirituality of the Third Millennium

Roger Lanphear

Third Millennium Spirituality
731 E Alejo Rd
Palm Springs CA 92262

Cover by Donald Lott

First published by Dog Ear Publishing
4010 W. 86th Street, Ste H
Indianapolis, IN 46268
www.dogearpublishing.net

ISBN: 978-160844-873-9

This paper is acid free and meets all ANSI standards for archival quality paper.
Printed in the United States of America

Table of Contents

Part III
The Foundation

Part IV
The Invocations

Part V
Wisdom and Practices

Part VI
Guiding Principles

ABOUT ROGER LANPHEAR

EDUCATION:

University of California, Berkeley: BS 1958

University of California, Berkeley: Juris Doctor 1961

PROFESSION: California Attorney from 1962 to 2006

PUBLISHED BOOKS:

Freedom From Crime, 1979, Nellen Publishing Co, NYC, NY (out of print)

Unified, 1987, DeVorss & Co, Publishers, Marina del Rey, CA Third printing 1991 (now out of print)

German Edition: Der Kurs zum Selbst, 1996 G. Reichel Verlag, Weilersbach, Germany

Dutch Edition: Eenheid, 2000, Petiet Uitgeverij Laren, The Netherlands

Love Consciousness, 2000, Author's Choice Press, an imprint of iUniverse,, Lincoln, NE

Health Consciousness, 2000, Author's Choice Press, an imprint of iUniverse,, Lincoln, NE (a reprint of Keep Your Self Alive, 1992)

German Edition: Erkenne Dich Und Du Bist Gesund, 2007, G. Reichel Verlag, Weilersbach, Germany

Wealth Consciousness, 2000, Author's Choice Press, an imprint of iUniverse,, Lincoln, NE (a reprint of Money Making , 1991)

Dutch Edition: Weelde Bewustzijn, 2003 Eenheid, Johan Gomers, The Netherlands

Preface

This is Holy Text. The words carry the key to heaven, nirvana, and enlightenment in this life without the need to die. Learn your connection to the almighty cosmos and what you already are: love, light, happiness, joy, bliss, all-knowing intelligence, everywhere present for all time, perfection, peace and gentleness, infinite energy, abundance, without judgment, and timeless.

Reading this book alone will not deliver the promised results. The words are merely the key to unlock the wisdom and qualities you have always owned. As you read each chapter, follow the instructions, much like you follow the words in a recipe book. After you have finished all chapters, go back to those practices and invocations you most resonate with. From time to time you will be attracted more to some than others. This is natural. Your intuition knows what to work on at the moment. Simply concentrate on the practices and invocations you are guided to, realizing you will naturally move around.

A bird builds its nest one straw at a time, not expecting the nest to be finished instantly. It is the same with this knowledge. Gradually layer upon layer is peeled back to expose who you are. You have tried countless approaches in this life and before. What a gift we now have to finally finish the task.

For only a few minutes each day, you can know and experience Who You Are. That is the goal of spirituality and the gift of the Third Millennium.

Part I
Introduction

The most beautiful thing we can experience is the mysterious. It is the source of all true art and science.

Albert Einstein

CHAPTER ONE
Holy Text—
The Link To Our Creator

At the beginning of each great period, supreme
knowledge appropriate for the time is brought forth.
We are entering a new millennium with the
consciousness of humanity leaping forward. As such,
this simple wisdom and these invocations and
practices have come forth. They are holy practices
because they link us to our Creator. This is supreme
knowledge—Holy Text.

Holy text is that which sets out the procedure for experiencing, remembering, and connecting to The Creator.

At different states of consciousness, different lessons are needed. "States of consciousness" is another way of stating the level of vibration. Everyone views life based on their level of vibration. For eons mankind on planet earth was stuck at a lower vibration, so the lessons had to be very elementary. The great religions of the world and their holy texts were limited by the consciousness of its followers.

In this, the third millennium AD, mankind's vibrations have increased. Greater clarity and understanding have dawned. New knowledge has been presented to experience, remember, and connect with The Creator. That brings a realization of our divinity as individual expressions of The Creator while remaining one with The Creator.

Part I: Introduction

These pages are truly Holy Text because they bring that new knowledge. They set out easy, simple procedures for experiencing, remembering, and connecting to The Creator. This knowledge not only transforms the life of every human, but leads each of us to experience the most elementary impulses of creative intelligence. Science labels those impulses Dark Matter and Dark Energy comprising about 95% of our universe.

The word "dark" does not imply anything sinister, but rather it means the Dark Matter and Dark Energy can't be seen in our universe. Light is not attracted to it and does not reflect off it. Dark Matter and Dark Energy actually attracts nothing and slips around without touching anything. It would go right through our visible creation without leaving a trace. This is the aspect of The Creator that creates. That is where all the qualities of The Creator can be experienced as your own. It is THE CREATIVE SOURCE of everything, and it is in that vastness where we are one with each other and all of creation.

It is true, as taught in all the great religions of earlier millenniums, that we are created in the image of The Creator. When we connect with The Creative Source we become aware that The Creator's qualities are our own. Any practice that gives us that experience is a holy practice opening our consciousness to know and feel our oneness with The Creator.

That is the gift of these pages, and why the simple words in this book are holy text. It is the definitive wisdom for the third millennium and beyond. Treat these pages with reverence, respect, and gratitude. Take this wisdom seriously.

Practice The Invocations. Live your life with the other daily practices. Digest the wisdom. Fill your life with love for all of The Creator's manifestations.

As you gain in your awareness of The Creative Source and The Creator, you will know the beauty and extent of your own reality. That is the gift of this wisdom, these invocations, and these practices. They take you to know your connection to the Creator, The Creative Source, the Almighty Cosmos, your Self, and all life forms.

That is why this is holy text.

Part I: Introduction

It is difficult to make a man miserable while he feels worthy of himself and claims kindred to the great God who made him.

Abraham Lincoln

CHAPTER TWO
Knowledge and Solutions

Knowledge is structured in consciousness. As our awareness and knowledge expands, deeper levels of the laws of nature are revealed. Rather than becoming more complex, the knowledge actually gets simpler. We are now to the point that whatever the problem, simple and easy solutions are ours for the asking.

It is simple. The solution is so simple.

Whatever the issues are in your life at the moment, the solution for coming to grips with them is simple. It is the same for the world. Solutions to the ills of human societies and their impact on the planet are also very simple.

We are neither going to spend chapters analyzing the problems nor even try to identify them. Whatever they are, there is a simple solution. This knowledge is timeless. The invocations and practices in this book are applicable to all human problems for all time—now as well as thousands of years from now.

We live on planet earth. We and this place are both a part of and one with the Almighty Cosmos. The one realization that science has taught and continues to teach is the perfect and predictable order of the entire system of worlds. The behavior of the tiniest subatomic particles, the simplest forms of cells, weather systems, the amazing combination of cells and organs for the

19

diversity of plants and animals, and the movement of planets, stars, galaxies are all perfectly ordered and predictable. The order even repeats itself. The largest systems appear to be a copy of the smallest, with nature imitating its own divine patterns.

Humanity has barely tapped into the knowledge of universal laws. As more of the laws of nature are revealed, the marvel of our creation becomes more and more astonishing—far beyond what is imaginable.

It is almost an axiom that as more knowledge is gained, the "knowledge" we know changes. Not long ago, we "knew" the sun went around the earth. It was even taught as divine truth in some religions. So as we gain more insight into the laws of nature, knowledge itself changes. Putting that another way, as our conscious awareness expands, knowledge appears different. Knowledge is structured in consciousness.

For instance, the concept of time as a constant has fallen apart. We now know time is different throughout the Universe, being a function of how an object moves through the cosmic ethers. Even the idea of measuring the distance of stars from us in light years becomes meaningless.

As humanity discovers more knowledge, that is, becomes more conscious, the wisdom of these simple invocations and practices you will learn in this book will make sense. In time, earth time, this is inevitable.

These invocations and practices have come to us before the scientific explanation of why they solve all problems. They need to come first, because they are the key to unlocking the mysteries of creation. All we need to do is learn to use that key.

As long as humans have been on the planet earth, wisdom and techniques for solving problems have been available. In each era, they are limited to the consciousness of the time. Each era has new techniques, each building on what came before. As the knowledge and consciousness advance, old techniques become archaic and more of a burden than help.

Now we are entering an era for techniques to be very easy and simple. The new ones replace techniques requiring hours of concentration, arduous physical exertion, and pure faith. It isn't that these techniques weren't valid. They were for their time. But now it is time to simplify and move on.

The wisdom, invocations, and practices in this book are the latest. They are universal. Any person of any religion will find them profound without interfering with any belief system. In fact, no beliefs are necessary, and believers of any religion will gain a deeper understanding of their religion with these invocations, practices, and wisdom. They unlock cosmic knowledge so that the truth behind all scriptures becomes clear and evident.

There is no need for suffering. There is no need to destroy our planet with human misuse. Suffering and destruction are not in the blueprint of the cosmos. We are now ready to step beyond suffering and destruction. The solution is now here.

There is no need to wonder where the wisdom, invocations, and practices came from. At some point that will be crystal clear. Then we will think, "Ah, of course. How could we have missed it." Just as we know now that the sun does not go around the earth (a no-brainer?), we now know how and why these are the solutions for creating nirvana, heaven, and utopia. And it is a no-brainer also.

Part II
The Nature of Creation

Enlighten the people, generally, and tyranny and oppressions of body and mind will vanish like spirits at the dawn of day.

Thomas Jefferson

CHAPTER THREE
Our Universe

Our Universe began with rapid oozing of Dark Matter/Dark Energy, the Unified Field, The Creative Source. Gradually the physical structure arose into billions of galaxies, each with billions of stars. It all began with the Creator's thought, and thought continues to shape all aspects of the physical world. The Universe's nature is to expand and eventually dissolve back to the source, a process carried on in an infinite number of other universes.

In the beginning of this Universe, there was great void—no space, no time, no atoms, no energy, not even a thought. As if coming from nowhere, as if oozing through a portal, great energy and great matter appears.

This energy and matter is without time or form, yet within it is all time and all form. It has particles, but nothing like the visible Universe we know. The particles are slippery, defying all rules of physics. In their natural state, they glide through each other as if neither exists. Yet they have infinite attraction.

In the early stage of our Universe, all that exists is this strange, indefinable matter and energy. As it oozes and expands it retains the same density and the same power. It can not be diluted.

As if by direction from an outside force, the particles combine to bring the first hint of our known Universe.

25

As great numbers of the first particles are born, an expansion takes place very rapidly. With the expansion, a solid block grows. Wildly separated new particles are swimming in the sea of the original matter and energy.

The continued expansion and more complex particles eventually give rise to light. This vibration and energy of light illumines the new creation without any effect on The Creative Source, the Unified Field, Dark Matter/Dark Energy. The Universe as we know it starts to take shape.

Because The Creative Source is timeless and without space as we know it, this Unified Field is not touched or influenced by its creation, whether just light in its many forms or physical matter. This "Source" remains invisible, undetectable, and dark.

From the perspective of those on earth, the expansion and individualization has continued for about fourteen billion years earth time. Arising entirely from The Creative Source, groupings of simple atoms of hydrogen and helium gradually become more and more complex. Clouds of variations of atoms and molecules give rise to form, eventually leading to stars and planets, then galaxies.

Today the expansion and complexity continues. Our own Sun with its planets and debris is a tiny part of creation arising from that first oozing of The Creative Source, the "Source". There are at least one hundred billion (100,000,000,000) other Suns in our galaxy. We now know there are at least another one hundred billion other galaxies with their own one hundred billion stars. It is a Universe so vast and complex that a human on earth finds it hard to comprehend.

Yes, quite amazing is this Universe. But even more amazing is that The Creative Energy, Dark Matter/Dark

Energy, still accounts for 96% of the stuff inside. It fills this Universe with the same density and power as it had in the first millisecond before the expansion began. It continues to be the "Source" of all creativity.

The Creative Source reacts to thought. It is a law of nature over which there is no alternative. Even the first stirrings were the result of great cosmic thought. Nothing is random or haphazard. The great cosmic thought gave rise to form from the abstract and incomprehensible The Creative Source, just as a potter shapes from clay.

The first impulse came from the One Great Mind. Then other great minds used their thought to shape and make matter in great and diverse environments, such to support life. Yes, it is thought and only thought that brought about our known, bright, light Universe. Even today great minds continue to shape galaxies and worlds.

In our own local world, the same principles are at work. Every individual on this planet is constantly shaping reality from The Creative Source from thoughts. It is the law. Everything begins with a thought, whether from the Great Cosmic Minds or from our own minds.

Since the Universe began with a great cosmic thought, that thought had to have come from somewhere. How could that thought effect The Creative Source unless it already existed as the first oozing? The answer is obvious. The oozing of The Creative Source, Dark Matter/Dark Energy, though timeless and without space, does exist beyond our Universe. It is as if a tiny pin prick opened up a leak from elsewhere to let in The Creative Source, so that the expansion and creation of the Universe could take place. But before the pin prick was made, a great cosmic thought started the process.

27

Outside our Universe is an infinite creation. We perceive our Universe as having boundaries—so many light years across, so many galaxies, so much time. However, our Universe is simply floating among a infinite others in a sea of creative intelligence. This degree of infinity is a strange, if not uncomfortable, concept for a dweller in finite space and a clear experience of time.

That whole infinite creation has its basis in the same Creative Source, which is that Unified Field, the Dark Matter/Dark Energy. It is the same "Source" as ours. Everywhere that "Source" responds to thought. Throughout this infinite creation, individual minds are creating their environments and experiences. Even though our Universe began oozing with the thought of one great cosmic mind, the process continues. First a few other great minds chimed in, then more, until now billions of minds on earth are thinking its future. Billions more are creating in other parts of our local Universe. And countless more are elsewhere, thinking and therefore creating.

Creation and dissolution is a natural law of nature. Our Universe began with the first oozing. It expanded and structure evolved. It continues to expand and differentiate. The expansion is now speeding up, and at some point our Universe will dissolve and return to The Creative Source. That is true for all Universes—a continual creation, expansion, and dissolution. That is the most fundamental law. However, nothing is ever lost in the dissolution.

CHAPTER FOUR
Our Selves

We are an expression of The Creative Source, the Unified Field, just as is all creation, including this Universe. The Unified Field responds to our thoughts, emotions, and intentions to deliver any experience we ask for. As such we need to monitor our thoughts, feelings, and intentions so they make us feel happy without any hint of lack.

We have a physical body in order to play and create on planet earth. The body locks us into time as experienced here and into this space, and into the vibration of visible light.

We could play and create anywhere there is Dark Energy/dark energy. In fact we are "that" Dark Energy and dark energy. Since "that" is outside of time and outside of location and space, we are also timeless and space-less in our ultimate reality. We can and do create and play in any time frame and at any place in creation.

Of course, we do experience time in a certain way while we are on earth. Elsewhere in creation time is not the same. It is not the same even elsewhere in our known Universe, as limited as that is. For instance, a lifetime here could be a day in another galaxy, or even elsewhere in our Milky Way. Being one with The Creative Source we are truly timeless and space-less— being able to experience all forms of time everywhere.

Being one with The Creative Source, we can melt into our source and be any place at any time at the speed of thought. While it would take billions of light years (earth time) to go across our Universe traveling at the speed of light, Dark Matter can deliver us anywhere at the speed of thought—that is, as fast as we can think of where we want to be. The Creative Source responds to thought and thought alone. Physical rules on planet earth are not relevant.

Since everything in creation is from The Creative Source, every soul is one with "that". We are all of the same source. We are all one, bound together and not as separate islands. That does not mean we are not individuals. We are indeed individuals, and we create our own reality with our thoughts, intentions, and emotions. Every one of our experiences are authored by us. While having individual experiences, we also create together with our mass-consciousness—what we think, intend, and feel together.

Being from The Creative Source, we are created outside of time. That means there is no time when we did not exist everywhere in creation. Our playground includes earth, but also everywhere else, even beyond our Universe.

We are created with all the gifts and powers of The Creative Source. None have been withheld. None! We are made in the image of that creator.

When death occurs to the physical body, you are just as complete as always. By letting go of the earth body, you are free to go any place and time of your choosing—meaning what your thoughts, intentions, and emotions have manifested. Subjectively that place and time can be experienced as good or bad, but nevertheless it is a place and time you brought about.

Since our thoughts, intentions, and emotions are the creating tools, we must be wise in managing and monitoring them. These muster The Creative Source and bring about our creation. All thoughts, not just carefully chosen affirmations, are signals of what we want. The Creative Source can only give us what we signal we want and will never turn us down.

Therefore, hold only thoughts, intentions, and emotions that make you happy. That is how to create your happy world. Whenever thoughts arise that are not happy, back off and substitute a thought that makes you feel happy.

Emotions are actually thoughts with more power. Feel the emotions of what you want in your life. Feel what it is like to have the love you want. Feel what it is like to have money. Feel what it is like to have perfect health. It is this feeling that sends the strong signal of what you want to have. This concept, more than any other, reveals who we really are and where our power resides.

Bad habits can interfere in this process. For instance, it is easy to get into a rut of feeling you haven't enough love, enough money, or good health. The slightest feeling of lack will bring about the experience of lack. Remember, The Creative Source delivers what is heard. If you feel lack, that will trump any words you utter, no matter how loud or long. The emotions of what you truly want must be there.

We fit perfectly in this Universe and all of Creation. We, like all other beings, create our experience. A "Great Thought" started this Universe by enlivening The

Creative Source. The same laws operate in each of our lives. Our thoughts also enliven The Creative Source.

This is who we are—timeless and space-less made in the image of our creator with powers to enliven The Creative Source for any experience we think, intend, and feel.

CHAPTER FIVE
Without Time and Space

*The Creative Source — the Unified Field — is without
time and space. We are one with that Unified Field
while dipping into time and space to play. At this time
we are locked into this earth, but in truth we belong to
the entire Creation of which this Universe is a part. We
have access to the entire Creation, all time, and all
space at the speed of thought.*

We are timeless. That is, we function in time and
also outside of time.

How could that be? It is because of the nature of
creation. The "in" and the "out". Oozing out of The
Creative Source is the stuff we see and identify with.
Time is within the structure from the tiniest impulses to
the great galaxies. While we play in this gigantic
playground, we play within time.

Time is found throughout this manifest Universe,
but it is not the same time throughout. The expansion of
the Universe creates the time. Without the expansion
there would be no time. Time results from relative
motion, that is two or more objects moving relative to
each other.

If you catch a ray of light and ride on it away from
the earth, time would be so different for you than your
friends on earth. In this extreme example time would be

a blink for you while earth people would have gone through eons of time.

In this same sense, time is different at different places in our Universe. Time would appear the same to two people billions of lights years apart. The difference is only noted if you compare the "years" at each place. A person on earth would experience a lifetime, while only a few hours could have passed for the other person a billion lights years away in another galaxy.

Time is the nature of the manifest Universe which resulted from the oozing of The Creative Source at the beginning of the Universe, the so-called big bang (although not a bang at all). Time, however, is not the property of the oozing of The Creative Source. Time came into existence as a characteristic of the stuff of the Universe. Twenty first century science identifies that "stuff" to represent only four percent, with the remaining ninety six percent being The Creative Source.

That would appear to be the case in the twenty first century and for the short term future. However, The Creative Source--Dark Matter/Dark Energy--maintains the same density in this expanded Universe as it did in the earlier, most compact stages. The Creative Source is without time and does not deal with space. It just is, and it maintains itself throughout the Universe, nay Creation, regardless of size. Therefore eons hence (earth time), the "stuff" of the manifest Universe will be less than four percent, and The Creative Source will appear to be more than its present ninety six percent.

"Space" is a characteristic of the manifest Universe only. Space has no meaning for The Creative Source. It only appears to have space because it seems to occupy every void between all things. Take the atom. It is mostly empty space—like a baseball in the middle of a soccer field, the nucleus is that ball surrounded by electrons on the perimeter of the field. What is in the void between the nucleus and electrons? The Creative Source.

For The Creative Source to fill the void, however, is just an appearance. In truth, it is everywhere and also nowhere. Not only is The Creative Source in all the voids, it is equally present within every manifested object, from the simplest vibration to the largest stars and galaxies.

There is no place where The Creative Source is not. That means it can't be located. It doesn't occupy a space because it is space-less. It gave rise to manifested Creation which is differentiated by the use of space. Only in the manifest form is there space.

The same is true of time. The Creative Source knows not time. Only in its manifest form does time appear, and time appears as a function of objects traveling through space.

The importance of understanding this nature of time and space is to throw light on our own nature. We are no different from all the rest of manifested Creation. We experience time and space, but the timeless/space-less Creative Source continues to underlie our being, as it does for everything else that is manifested. We cannot disconnect from that source, so we are deeply rooted in timelessness without space.

That playground of Creation, our Universe, is fun. It is a perpetual vacation. It is made for our enjoyment and to experience the fullness of life. Without such a playground, existence would be dull to say the least.

The fact that The Creative Source continues to permeate every aspect and particle of our being brings profound realizations. Since we are ultimately timeless and space-less (yet playing in time and space), we have no beginning and no end. That is immortality, the grandest scheme of all. We never can lose our oneness with The Creative Source. We flow in and out of it constantly. Popping up here, then there, with each time and space taking on a new physical body to lock us in.

On planet earth in the twenty first century many beings have popped up for various reasons. Some came because of the opportunities present to wake up their full and true Self. Some came to help in that awakening. Whatever the reason for being on earth, each person is equal and one with The Creative Source. The only difference is how each perceives that realization.

Interestingly enough, some beings came from afar and live a lifetime as teachers or as antennas to focus knowledge and energy. Because time is different at different places in the Universe, the lifetime here could be but a night's rest someplace else. Imagine waking up after dropping the earth body and saying to your beloved, "Wow, what a dream!".

Such travel instantaneously from here to any place in the Universe is simple because we are one with The Creative Source. We melt into it, and at the speed of thought can be someplace else. No time or space is experienced. We just use our trait of timelessness without space for instant travel.

This is our experience in this manifested Universe, which is our home now. There are others, in fact infinite other environments. Some will be like a heaven. Some will be like a hell. All, however, are what we have created for our own experience in the playgrounds of time and space.

36

Since this Universe is our present home in time and space, it appears that we had a beginning here after it was manifested, and that we will end when the Universe expands to such an extent it folds back into The Creative Source. That is not the case. We are one with the limitless, timeless Creative Source without space which permeates all of creation, not just this Universe. We never began and we never end. We simply dip into time and space to play forever, without beginning and without end.

The thought manifests as the word;
The word manifests as the deed;
The deed develops into habit;
And habit hardens into character;
So watch the thought and its ways with care,
And let it spring from love
Born out of concern for all beings...
As the shadow follows the body,
As we think, so we become.
Buddha

CHAPTER SIX
Diversity of Life

*The life force is everywhere present. It exists at all
levels of vibration, at every place in our Universe and
beyond. The infinite variety of forms is unimaginable,
yet all come from the one Source, the Unified Field. Life
cannot be created, nor destroyed. Our humility requires
us to honor all life, as being one with us.*

As openers, there is only one life force. It has its
roots in The Creative Source. We are all one, all
connected, all with the life sustaining qualities of that
Almighty Source. For all life there is no end and no
beginning. Life with its individual consciousness cannot
be killed, although it can disappear from view.

All of that life force permeates all of our manifest
Universe, indeed all of Creation. All life has equal access
to the entire Creation, all life has always been alive and
conscious before it appears in our manifest Universe.

Life force manifests in infinite forms. It exists in the
most simple of vibration and the most complex. It exists
within life forms, such as cells and organs, which
themselves are alive with consciousness. Life exists
where it would seem impossible, like in the middle of a
rock or within a lava flow. There is literally nowhere in

39

Creation, let alone our Universe, where life force is absent.

Furthermore life appears at all vibrations, layer upon layer. We now experience life in the layer of visible light so we narrowly look for it only at that level. At the vibration of ultra violet or of x-ray, we do not notice life. We simply don't have the tools to perceive or recognize it, even if we believed it could be there.

We could hop onto a fast vehicle and go to a distant planetary system and see nothing. It would be barren to us. Yet at a level we don't perceive, that barren place could be teeming with life.

Even at our visible light level life is more complex than a first impression reveals. We can see that within our bodies live seemingly infinite variations. Each cell has its function and consciousness. Within our bodies live billions of other beings in the form of viruses, microbes, antibodies, hormones, and on and on. Each has a life, and purpose, and consciousness.

As humans we form communities, and these take on a form of life with mass-consciousness. Then there is "Mother Earth", aware and alive. "She" is part of a solar system with its planets, moons, asteroids, and other matter. That is alive, conscious, and aware.

The solar system joins other such beings to become a galaxy—again alive, aware, and conscious. These are ever changing, as is all life. Sometimes the galaxies "marry" and join to become one. Clusters of galaxies also form a life force, of which our own Universe is one mighty life that is alive, aware, and conscious.

That description of life only deals with life at the level of visible light. That is such a small part of life, even here in this Universe. It is only the portion we see and understand. The complexity of life becomes mind boggling at other levels. Life is teeming around us, right in our space and time, yet we are unaware of those other levels. A few people can get glimpses from time to time, but for the most part the other levels are far removed from our observation.

The infinity of life in our Universe is just a drop in the bucket of life for all Creation. Remember, our Universe is but one of many such playgrounds. While we are here, our Universe is our home. At any time we can reenter The Creative Source and reinvent ourselves somewhere else. Generally that "somewhere else" is within our Universe, but we are not restricted. We are one with all life, and that life permeates all Creation with its infinite Universes.

Life likes to cluster. The human family is such a cluster. We have a group life and group consciousness. Within that large humanity cluster are smaller families that tend to hang out together. That is our spiritual family. We come and go with each other, life after life, sometimes on earth for ages, sometimes moving around our Universe, or even other parts of Creation. Bonds between people are strong, and we flow together like a packed school of fish.

PART II The Nature of Creation

Our bodies are our gardens to which our wills are gardeners.

William Shakespeare

Part III
The Foundation

Always aim at complete harmony of thought and word and deed. Always aim at purifying your thoughts and everything will be well.

Mahatma Gandhi

CHAPTER SEVEN
Thoughts and Actions

*Every action, thought, feeling, and intention of ours
goes out into creation coded with our unique vibration.
That impulse returns to us magnified. What we send
out, we get back in like form—love for love, pain for
pain. We are created outside of time, but came on earth
to live in time. All that comes to us in life is a result of
our returning impulses, whether sent out in this
lifetime or another.*

The great teachings of the world deal with some
aspect of "cause and effect". "Every action creates a
reaction." "An eye for an eye." "As you sow, so shall
you reap." "The law of karma." Religious leaders, great
philosophers, and scientists recognize that what happens is a result of what preceded it.

Not clearly understood, however, is the extent and
accuracy of this principle. Every moment of every
minute we create our future. If you wonder what you
are creating, you only have to observe your present
situation.

It is clear that actions lead to reactions. Poke
someone in the nose, and you might get poked back or
go to jail. But what if you get away with the poke?
Doesn't that prove not all actions lead to reactions? No,
it doesn't.

We all have a unique vibration. You can often feel that vibration when you are around someone. The person's vibration can be attractive or repulsive, and we can all sense that. Everyone has their unique coded vibration, and it attaches to every action. Then an impulse (containing the memory of the action and your coded vibration) is sent out into the cosmic ethers, and it comes back magnified. It returns home to the actor by seeking out its own vibration, wherever the person is and in whatever time period.

Everything you do comes back to you amplified. Usually what comes back is not recognized as being a result of your action. If you poke someone, it won't return as a poke. In the case of a destructive action, what returns is not going to be fun or comfortable. More than likely, it will come in the form of suffering. This is a basic law of nature. You send out; you get back a likeness. It is enjoyable or suffering, depending entirely upon what you created.

Isn't this cruel? How could a cosmos that is perfect, gentle, and even loving inflict such pain? Shouldn't there be a universal forgiveness? The Universe makes no judgment, and your free will is protected above all else. You can create whatever you want. However, the Universe nudges toward spiritual growth. The universal law is structured to aid in such growth, to expand knowledge, to receive and give love, and to recognize oneness and perfection.

When you poke someone in the face, don't you show you're missing the point? Don't you show you need some instruction? Don't you need some judging? The "Great Teacher" doesn't just give you a lecture, although that could happen if you knew how to listen.

Being "deaf", the teaching comes in the form of an experience. Hopefully the experience will lead to more empathy, understanding, and love. Whether it does or not is your free choice.

Nature pushes for a correction as soon as possible, but if you don't "get it", more lessons will come as you set up new situations by your own actions.

It isn't just negative actions that come back. All actions do. A loving gesture to a stranger or an unsolicited smile returns magnified with many rewards. Give a dime to a stranger, and you'll be rewarded many fold. The gift to you might be a smile from someone, or it might come in the form of money found in the street. Chances are you won't make the connection. All acts of kindness, love, and support return to make your life incredibly rewarding. If that isn't your experience, examine your actions.

Actually, always examine your actions. Your actions are strong and always return to you with great potency. However, it isn't just actions. Every thought also attached to your coded vibration, goes out, gains amplitude, and returns. Every intention, whether acted on or not, comes back. Every feeling also goes out and comes back.

This is simple knowledge that has been known for eons. It is not even a new idea for you. Intuitively you've always known that everything you do, think, intend, or feel sets up your future. That means your present circumstances are a result of your past thoughts, actions, intentions, and emotions.

All religions teach that man is a soul apart from the body. When the soul is created is debated. However, since science knows that absolute time does not exist, it is easy to think of a soul being created outside of time but being able to function within time.

We experience time on planet earth, but we also exist outside of time. We did not begin our journey at a certain time, but came to earth to experience earth time and space. To lock ourselves into earth's time and space, we took on an earth body—earth's "space suit". When we came, we came with our original coded vibration. All the past actions, thoughts, intentions, and emotions that had not returned to us, do return, either as opportunities for growth or rewards. The unfairness and disparity is hardly random or an accident. All the "cause and effect" was already in operation at birth.

This concept of life before birth for an individual soul may be difficult to grasp at first. It is not necessary to accept or believe this. At some point these concepts will appear self evident, and you'll understand why some people seem to be so disadvantaged at birth.

The important lesson to learn here is to learn to monitor your thoughts, your actions, your intentions, and your emotions. When you see negativity creeping in, disavow it. Whenever your thoughts do not give happy feelings, go to a thought that does. It could be as simple as enjoying scenery or thinking about someone you love. Change your direction. Not to do so is foolish, especially since you have been introduced to the effect of whatever you do, think, intend, or feel.

In the next chapter you will learn brand new knowledge—that is, new if you're reading this in the beginning of the twenty first century. THE INVOCATIONS start the process of neutralizing and obliterating all those vibrations out there that interfere with a happy, abundant, and healthy life.

MONITOR THYSELF

Pay attention to your actions. If any appear to show anger, jealousy, revenge, hatred, mockery, or anything not loving, back off and start over.

Monitor your thoughts. If you catch yourself with less than loving thoughts, change the thought and intentionally correct it. Have thoughts that make you happy. Let the feeling of happiness be your guide.

Intend only what is in your best interest and the best interest of everyone around you. If you find yourself intending less, reword and rethink that intention.

Come to grips with your emotions. Do not harbor ill feelings toward anyone, and try to feel love. No matter how hard that may be, at least say to yourself the emotion you want to feel.

Know that what you do, think, intend, and feel will return to you. Knowing that is the incentive to monitor yourself and change accordingly.

CHAPTER EIGHT
The Universal Connection

This is a Simple Meditation that brings us back to The Creative Source—the Unified Field, that most subtle vibration from which all in creation arises. That connection allows us to harvest the riches available for all life, but from which many of us have been separated. The practice is simple, foolproof, and impossible to misuse. It is to be practiced twice daily for twenty minutes, and it is the foundation for all the invocations and practices that are to follow in this book.

You are now going to learn THE UNIVERSAL CONNECTION, a simple meditation. This is the foundation for all solutions. The foundation is "universal" for two reasons. It is for all people, regardless of race, wealth, station, religion, beliefs, body type, color, size, or age. And it applies to the Universe. That is, THE UNIVERSAL CONNECTION connects and reconnects each person to the powers, knowledge, and promises of the Almighty Universe to which we all belong.

THE UNIVERSAL CONNECTION is important because it establishes the link to the most elementary aspect of our Universe, thus creating the power for the invocations and practices to work. It is like a phone or internet connection.

51

THE UNIVERSAL CONNECTION is to be used as a prelude to all the invocations and practices that follow. Furthermore, it is an invaluable practice alone. Connecting to the Universe once or twice daily for twenty minutes, or so, opens and strengthens your bond to all that is. Without any other technique or practice, THE UNIVERSAL CONNECTION alone leads to more perfect health, prosperity, rewarding relationships, peace of mind, wisdom, reliable intuition, and an easy flow through life. With time all this, and more, becomes your reality.

THE UNIVERSAL CONNECTION is the beanstalk that grows and grows and takes you to utopia, the concept of heaven, the promised land of all religions for all time. THE INVOCATIONS in the following chapters are the fertilizer that magnify the growth. They transform the beanstalk from a seedling to a giant stalk in no time, actually outside of time. Like Jack who climbed the beanstalk to retrieve the pot of gold, all riches of almighty creation are the reward of THE UNIVERSAL CONNECTION.

As you practice THE UNIVERSAL CONNECTION daily, its benefits and rewards become obvious in everyday life. You would find it fun to keep a journal of changes you note. Whether it be improved health, "ah-ha" glimpses, unexplained prosperity, or general feelings, make note of them. As life changes, we tend to forget the process, so your notes can verify and document your progress with THE UNIVERSAL CONNECTION.

THE UNIVERSAL CONNECTION is simple. It requires no effort and no knowledge. In fact, the more innocent you are, the easier it is.

Begin by sitting comfortably. Close your eyes, and allow your attention to be with your breath. In a few moments, connect your breathing. That is, there is no space between the in and the out breaths. Your breath is like a huge wheel, just going around and around.

Continue the connected breathing for a few minutes. If you notice a movement of the head or your torso—like a swaying to and fro—start breathing normally and allow your attention to be with the movement. If after a few sessions you do not notice the movement of the head or your torso, gently let your head move from side to side. It will find its own rhythm.

Whether you're connecting your breath or noticing the movement, ignore your thoughts. Allow them to be there. Do not try to remove thoughts. Simply allow your attention to be with the connected breath or the slight movements of your head or torso.

This is THE UNIVERSAL CONNECTION. It connects you to the universal vibration, also known in physics as the Unified Field. It is the vibration from which all of creation arises.

To become aware of—to consciously connect to—the universal vibration that underlies all of creation is the single most significant accomplishment you can make in life. From there springs the solution to all problems.

Practice THE UNIVERSAL CONNECTION for twenty minutes or so in the morning and evening. If you find that difficult to maintain, you may think of any of the chants you have learned in your religion, along with awareness of your breathing and the head or torso movement.

After you are comfortable with THE UNIVERSAL CONNECTION, then go on to the next chapter to start learning the invocations and practices.

THE UNIVERSAL CONNECTION

Sit comfortably with connected breathing.

Change to normal breathing if you notice a swaying of your head or your torso.

If you wish, you may think a chant from your culture.

Ignore thoughts; don't try to erase them or deal with them.

Continue for about twenty minutes.

Part IV
The Invocations

The great majority of us are required to live a life of constant, systematic duplicity. Your health is bound to be affected if, day after day, you say the opposite of what you feel, if you grovel before what you dislike and rejoice at what brings you nothing but misfortune. Our nervous system isn't just a fiction, it's part of our physical body, and our soul exists in space and is inside us, like teeth in our mouth. It can't be forever violated with impunity.

Boris Pasternak (from Doctor Zhivago)

CHAPTER NINE
The Invocation for Prosperity

*To manifest prosperity we need to monitor our actions,
thoughts, emotions, and intentions, and we need to
connect to the Unified Field—The Creative Source. We
can burn away past thoughts, emotions, and intentions
that are bound to bring poverty, and we can reprogram
our subconscious mind so we stop automatically
sending out such impulses, thus nipping the poverty in
the bud.*

Poverty is not a concept known to Almighty
Creation. Infinity is its hallmark. Smaller than the tiniest
and larger than the greatest, creation abounds in
abundance.

How is it then that people can experience lack of the
physical requirement for an abundant life? The answer
is simple: that is what the person manifested for himself
or herself.

Give a person steeped in poverty a gift of money,
even a large sum, and chances are the person will return
to poverty. Take away the wealth of a person steeped in
abundance, and chances are the person will regain a life
of abundance. It all happens seemingly without any
conscious thought. It appears automatic and seems
unfair.

The cosmos is not unfair. To the contrary the cosmos
is available for our every wish. There are two natural

laws intended to bring prosperity, but are misused to create poverty.

The first natural law we have already discussed: every action, thought, intent, and emotion come back to its source, returning the same experience magnified. For every action there is a resulting reaction. Every one of us experiences this law of nature, and there is no way to avoid it. However, there is seldom a connection made by our intellect relating the action and the reaction. Some of what comes back to us is related to abundance or lack of it. What was sown determines the harvest.

A vicious cycle can create the experience of poverty or any other undesirable experience. Anger, jealousy, revenge, and such thoughts and emotions create the undesirable reaction, which then creates more anger, jealousy, and revenge. It goes on and on in an endless circle.

Every person needs to be aware of this law of nature. If we do nothing else but monitor our thoughts, actions, intentions, and emotions so that we send out into the ethers life supporting impulses, our lives will change.

The second natural law is that we create at the most simple, most subtle vibration—the Unified Field. We are all capable of using that first stirring of The Creative Source to manifest. The experience of poverty only proves the connection to this field is lost. Not being connected to that field shuts out our greatest tool for experiencing prosperity. All the affirmations and prayers go unheard, like yelling into a dead telephone.

To gain your rightful inheritance from the cosmos, you must deal with these two laws. Until recently they were not understood by most. Even those people who knew of these laws found it an uphill struggle to always send out life supporting impulses and to stay connected to the Unified Field. No longer. New knowledge and new techniques are now available for every person to allow these laws to work for them.

THE UNIVERSAL CONNECTION is one aspect of this new knowledge. The repeated practice strengthens and repairs your connection to the Unified Field. Eventually the connection is restored, allowing the manifesting powers of nature to work for you. When your connection to the Unified Field is complete, another benefit matures: actions, thoughts, intention, desires, and emotions arise that are totally life supporting. Only that which is in your highest and wisest interest appears. That means that what you send out, comes back intensified with life support goodness packed with prosperity. This is why THE UNIVERSAL CONNECTION is extremely important and is to be practiced twice daily.

In addition to THE UNIVERSAL CONNECTION— that simple meditation, you need to learn and practice THE INVOCATION FOR PROSPERITY. This invocation neutralizes your actions, thoughts, intentions, and emotions that are returning to give you the experience of poverty and lack. This invocation has always been available, but until recently had been forgotten. It is your birthright, and it is very simple.

After twenty minutes of THE UNIVERSAL CONNECTION, you simply imagine a flame, the color of violet, burning and whirling around your body. As it burns and whirls, know that it is burning away and neutralizing the unwanted cycle before it returns to you with unwanted poverty and lack. While imagining this, think or speak out the equivalent of these words:

"Using this , I welcome all the forces of Almighty Nature, from every level of vibration, and from every realm, and request that the effects of my inappropriate thoughts, actions, intentions, and emotions that interfere with my experience of prosperity are burned and destroyed before they can return to me. I further request that any subconscious thoughts I have that are inconsistent with my prosperity be erased and replaced by appropriate and life supporting subconscious thoughts. From now on the violet flame shall monitor my subconscious thoughts and my outgoing impulses and shall correct them so they are only in accordance with my highest good."

You can do this invocation as often as you want, but more than once is truly not necessary. It needs to be performed only once with the feelings and emotions. Then whatever stands in the way of your prosperity is gone. Just don't think or feel poverty or lack to start the process over again.

THE INVOCATION FOR PROSPERITY

20 minutes of THE UNIVERSAL CONNECTION—the simple meditation.

Visualize a flame, violet in color, whirling and flaming around your body.

Think or speak out the equivalent of these words:

"I invite all the forces of Almighty Nature, from every level of vibration, and from every realm, to destroy and eliminate from my life the effects of my inappropriate thoughts, actions, intentions, and emotions that interfere with my experience of prosperity. I further request that any subconscious thoughts I have that are inconsistent with my prosperity be erased and replaced by appropriate and life supporting subconscious thoughts. From now on the violet flame shall monitor my subconscious thoughts and my outgoing impulses and shall correct them so they are only in accordance with my highest good."

*Get not your friends by bare compliments, but by
giving them sensible tokens of your love.*

Socrates

CHAPTER TEN
The Invocation for Perfect Health

Our human body is more than we can see. It consists of layer upon layer, reaching all the way to the Unified Field where everything is one. It is perfect, and each layer is self correcting to maintain that perfection. By invoking the violet flame , we can burn away disease laden thoughts, emotions, and intentions before they return to us, and we can reprogram our subconscious mind to inhibit other such thoughts, emotions, and intentions from arising.

THE INVOCATION for opening yourself up to abundance must seem naively simple. How could a technique so simple be so potent? It is because we have reached a critical point in human evolution. Energies from the cosmos have opened for our use. Unseen forces of nature are at work to give us the tools we need for full spiritual growth.

In all cultures, there are stories about how mankind fell from grace. This is when the connection to the creative vibration of the Unified Field was severed. Without that connection, suffering and poverty were manifested. To reconnect simply takes doing THE UNIVERSAL CONNECTION and invoking these unseen forces. Skepticism won't deter the results. Even disbelief won't negate the power. It only takes the intention to follow the procedure. All else is automatic.

The invocation to gain perfect health is similar to the invocation for abundance. We are created to enjoy a healthy body. Not to have it is not part of the cosmic plan. It isn't necessary to know all about the way nature plans for and delivers healthy bodies. It is suffice to know it would appear complicated, with layer upon layer of the unseen. Those layers are always there, but we have divorced ourselves from their management.

THE INVOCATION FOR PERFECT HEALTH to reestablish the connection to those layers to have perfect health is simple—of course. Begin with THE UNIVERSAL CONNECTION for twenty minutes. Then imagine a bright violet flame whirling over your head; then over your forehead; then over your throat; then over your heart; then over your stomach; then at the base of your spine; and finally between your feet. At each point think or speak out the equivalent of the following words:

"I invoke the power of Almighty Creation, with all the unseen energies and cosmic beings to bring perfect health. I invite new subconscious thoughts to replace any thoughts I have—known or unknown—that interfere with perfect health. I also declare that any inappropriate thoughts, actions, intentions, and emotions that I have ever had or experienced be neutralized and burned so they cannot return to me. From now on the violet flame shall monitor my subconscious thoughts and my outgoing impulses and shall correct them so they are only in accordance with my highest good."

You can read these words or memorize them. Or you can use your own to invite new subconscious thoughts and to neutralize inappropriate actions, thoughts, intentions, and emotions before they return to

64

you. Most important is that you visualize the flame with healing intent.

After your twenty minutes of THE UNIVERSAL CONNECTION, you can do the invocation for both prosperity and for perfect health, back to back, as often as you want. However, do not do them again and again because you doubted it had worked. Each invocation works and there is no need to repeat it. Doubt or disbelief interferes with your intention to do the invocation for its desired results.

THE INVOCATION FOR PERFECT HEALTH

Twenty minutes of THE UNIVERSAL CONNECTION.

Visualize the violet flame whirling around these parts of your body: head; forehead; throat; heart; stomach; base of spine; and feet.

Think or speak out the equivalent of the following words:

"I invoke the power of Almighty Creation, with all the unseen energies and heavenly beings to bring perfect health. I invite new subconscious thoughts to replace any thoughts I have—known or unknown— that interfere with perfect health. I also declare that any inappropriate thoughts, actions, intentions, and emotions that I have ever had or experienced be neutralized so they not return to me. From now on the violet flame shall monitor my subconscious thoughts and my outgoing impulses and shall correct them so they are only in accordance with my highest good."

CHAPTER ELEVEN
The Invocation for Loving Relationships

There are two instructions for loving relationships.
First, think four sentences with someone in mind: I give
you my love; I give you my heart; I accept your love; I
accept your heart. Second, we can burn away our past
thoughts, emotions, and intentions that create
relationship problems. The same invocation
reprograms our subconscious mind so we attract love.

Dealing with people is one of our greatest challenges, or so it seems. Wherever we turn, there are people to deal with. Some are our intimate friends or partners. Others we know from work. Others are in our close support group, while most are part of the background. Whatever the relationship, we must deal with people constantly.

That is the third major category in life offering an avenue for growth. Just like coming to grips with prosperity and health, relationships are major concerns. The purpose of this chapter is to learn how to smooth out the experience of people so we can have everyone augment the feeling of love.

An invaluable practice is called THE LOVE CONNECTION. Think of someone with these words in your thoughts:

I give you my love;

I give you my heart;

I receive your love;

I receive your heart.

Then back off a few moments and feel the love connect with that person. It wells up in pulsations of love emanating from your heart.

THE LOVE CONNECTION is helpful when there is tension with someone. It can be a stranger in a crowded room who rubbed you the wrong way. It can be an overbearing work boss or associate. Or the tension could arise over an argument with a spouse. In every situation with tension, thinking these words, then backing off, melts away the problem.

You can also think these words about someone with whom you already feel deep unconditional love. The words augment the feelings and open your heart wider. In the case where a loved one has died, the words promote healing, not to make you forget, but to rid you of the pain. The same healing can take place in situations of breakups or divorce. The words evoke the feelings of love, which is the master healer. In that regard these words practiced regularly deliver benefits in all areas of your life, including prosperity and health. They are truly magical. You cannot think them too often.

These words are also important because they are thoughts you're sending into the cosmos. Remember, every thought returns to you magnified. By sending out these thoughts, not only will you have immediate benefit, but when they return, the dividends of love are multiplied.

People with relationship challenges and difficulties can't blame other people. The difficulties are simply the return of past actions, thoughts, intentions, and emotions. Stopping the return of all that is inappropriate from the past is essential to eliminate toxic relationships and painful situations with people. THE LOVE CONNECTION goes miles in neutralizing the effects, but you also need THE INVOCATION FOR RELATIONSHIPS. It is the same basic invocation we used for prosperity and health.

After twenty minutes or so of THE UNIVERSAL CONNECTION, focus on your heart. Visualize the violet flame whirling around, in, and through your heart, and think the equivalent of these words:

"I give love to all the people I have acted in a cruel way toward, thought evil about, intended to harm, and felt anger toward. I forgive all people whom I feel have hurt or harmed me in any way, by sending them love. I ask that the flame burn and neutralize all impulses I have sent out that could return to me causing toxic and difficult relationships. I ask that the flame burn away all unconscious thoughts that are harmful to my relationships or inappropriate in any way and substitute life affirming and loving thoughts that can only bring love into my life. All my past that was harmful in any way is now burned in this flame. From now on the violet flame shall monitor my subconscious thoughts and my outgoing impulses and shall correct them so they are only in accordance with my highest good."

Again, this sounds simplistic. Yet it is the most profound thing you can do to improve your relationships. You can't experience the full value of love without experiencing the love of all the people around you.

These three techniques for prosperity, health, and relationships are all connected. It is like pulling one leg on a chair. The other legs follow. Perfect health affects your relationships and your prosperity. Prosperity affects your health and relationships. And relationships influence health and prosperity. They are really all the same.

You can practice THE INVOCATION FOR RELATIONSHIPS along with the other invocations. Do them together or alternate. The important point is that twice every day spend twenty minutes with THE UNIVERSAL CONNECTION, followed by THE LOVE CONNECTION and if you want, one or all of the invocations, remembering that they are complete each time.

THE LOVE CONNECTION

Think of someone with these words in your thoughts:

I give you my love;

I give you my heart;

I receive your love;

I receive your heart.

Then back off a few moments and feel the love connect with that person. It wells up in pulsations of love emanating from your heart.

THE INVOCATION FOR RELATIONSHIPS

Twenty minutes of THE UNIVERSAL CONNECTION.

Focus on your heart.

Visualize the violet flame whirling around, in, and through your heart.

Think the equivalent of these words:

"I give love to all the people I have acted in a cruel way toward, thought evil about, intended to harm, and felt anger toward. I forgive all people whom I feel have hurt or harmed me in any way, and I send them love. For all unconscious thoughts that are harmful to me or inappropriate in any way, I now erase those thoughts and substitute life affirming and loving thoughts. All my past that was harmful in any way is now burned in this flame. From now on the violet flame shall monitor my subconscious thoughts and my outgoing impulses and shall correct them so they are only in accordance with my highest good."

CHAPTER TWELVE
Specific Invocations

We can create an invocation for any conceivable purpose in our lives. For health, we can focus on organs or diseases. For abundance, we can focus on specific elements, like career, skills, or balance. For relationships, we can focus on sex, communication, or family. Quality of life needs are endless: laughter, leisure, talents, and joy. Even spirituality can have specific invocations: telepathy, self awareness, and knowledge of nature. Whatever we need, we can invoke.

THE INVOCATIONS for perfect health, for abundance, and for meaningful relationships are just a hint of the limitless possibilities when invoking the flame. That flame, violet in color, when invoked, changes all aspects of your life that can interfere with living a life as it is intended to be lived.

THE INVOCATIONS you're learned so far are broad brush strokes. They are generic, dealing in a general way with health, prosperity, and relationships. While extremely valuable in that form, you can narrow the focus for as many invocations as you can imagine.

In dealing with health matters, you can invoke the flame for specific illnesses or body parts. After all, whatever the ailment, it is a result of a returned thought, action, intention, or emotion. They are seldom remembered and certainly not connected to the ailment.

73

Nevertheless, the violet flame will neutralize all the energy returning to you causing the illness. At the same time, remember to monitor your actions, thoughts, intentions, and emotions so you don't repeat the cycle. Always be in a space of love regardless of the circumstances. If thoughts are making you unhappy, slide over to a happy thought.

You can focus THE INVOCATION for specific organs: eyes, the heart, the liver, the intestines, back, arms, and so on. You can focus THE INVOCATION for specific diseases: heart disease, hepatitis, intestinal problems, muscle disorders, virus and germ infections, glaucoma, or any conceivable condition. This works because when you are connected to the Unified Field using THE UNIVERSAL CONNECTION, imagining and invoking the flame returns your body to its natural, originally designed state.

Besides focusing on specific health concerns, you can also focus on perfect eating, drinking, and exercise habits. You can include an invocation for balance between work and recreation, living with perfect leisure time activities. You can invoke peacefulness, peace of mind, and an anxiety free day, the lack of which sets up toxic actions, thoughts, intentions, and emotions—the root of the problems.

You can expand your invocations in dealing with prosperity. You can focus on the most rewarding career, having ideal work habits, following your life purpose, or developing creative skills. It is usually not best to focus on a specific job, but rather to be guided to the job or for having it naturally unfold.

In manifesting prosperity, it is wise to invoke balance. All work and no play does not lead to enjoyable abundance. Use the invocation to invoke fun, recreation, and child-like play. You will soon discover that these have a special role in delivering abundance. It isn't just work.

Likewise, there are infinite ways to invoke perfect relationships. Invoke the violet flame for a wonderful family life, clear communication, exciting and rewarding sex life, and to be guided to the perfect people. It is best not to go after a particular person. That attempts to interfere with their life and destiny, which you can not do anyway. Instead focus on allowing the perfect people to come and then be welcome into your life.

Quality of life has countless components. Think of the ones that you seem to be lacking and invoke the flame. Here are some examples: laughter, child like joy, easy enthusiasm, a sense of wonderment, and feelings of peace mixed with tireless energy. Develop your creative self by invoking your talent for music, art, dancing, or writing.

While you're thinking about the infinite possibilities for invoking the flame, don't forget your spiritual qualities. Invoke the flame to gain telepathic communication with all beings, including the animal kingdom and whether seen or unseen. Invoke for your feelings of reverence for all life. Invoke your ability to know the laws of nature, even those that seem unknowable. Invoke for your understanding of who you are and how you fit into space and time, as well as beyond space and time. Above all, invoke to discover your perfect spiritual path, of which there are many.

THE INVOCATIONS for the infinite variations begin with twenty minutes or so of THE UNIVERSAL CONNECTION—that simple meditation. Then visualize a flame, violet in color, whirling around your whole body. When you feel centered with the flame, think the equivalent of these words:

"I invoke the violet flame to achieve _____. All my inappropriate thoughts, actions, intentions, and emotions are burned and neutralized, whatever or whenever their origin. For any subconscious thoughts that I have that interfere with achieving _____, I invoke the flame to erase and substitute the correct life supporting subconscious thoughts in their place. From now on the violet flame shall monitor my subconscious thoughts and my outgoing impulses and shall correct them so they are only in accordance with my highest good."

You may read this, or you may think it or speak it out in your own words. Then back off for a few moments and feel love well up as changes take place.

SPECIFIC INVOCATION

Begin with twenty minutes or so with THE UNIVERSAL CONNECTION.

Then visualize the violet flame whirling around your whole body.

Think or speak out the equivalent of the following:

*"I invoke the violet flame to achieve _____.
All my inappropriate thoughts, actions, intentions, and emotions are neutralized, whatever or whenever their origin. For any subconscious thoughts that I have that interfere with achieving _____, I invoke the flame to erase and substitute the correct life supporting thoughts in their place. From now on the violet flame shall monitor my subconscious thoughts and my outgoing impulses and shall correct them so they are only in accordance with my highest good."*

Back off and feel love well up as the changes take place.

Our doubts are traitors.
William Shakespeare

CHAPTER THIRTEEN
Invocation for Humanity

*We are all One, emanating from the Unified Field
which we hold in common. As such, an invocation for
humanity can change everyone's destiny. It burns and
erases pain inducing thoughts, emotions, and
intentions from manifesting. It reprograms the
subconscious minds of all people, so only loving
impulses are released to return magnified. We can
create an invocation for small groups or the whole of
humanity. We can create invocations for specific needs.
The result is to raise consciousness and enliven the
feelings of love for everyone.*

We are all one. All religions teach this oneness. We
are individual expressions, all arising from an all
encompassing Almighty Force which ranges from
smaller than the smallest imaginable to greater than the
greatest imaginable. It is this connection to the Unified
Field, The Creative Source, which marries all our
destinies.

You cannot expand your conscious awareness
without raising everyone else's to some degree. When
you expand your awareness, your consciousness, the
natural result brings harmony between individuals,
among families, among nations, and globally. There are
no ethnic, color, regional, or national boundaries. We are
all one.

Because of that oneness, we can use the invocations for the benefit of others. THE INVOCATION FOR HUMANITY is the same you have already learned with the added intention of including other people. Intention is the key.

When you do so, keep in mind that you can not interfere with another person's free will. If it is not their will to receive the benefits of the invocations, they will not. However, if they have the slightest desire to come to grips with the issues dealt with in the invocation, your help will be enormous.

Also keep in mind that THE INVOCATION FOR HUMANITY will only deliver what that soul determines to be in his or her highest and wisest interest. No harm can result. Any perceived harm could only result from the person's own making.

You can offer THE INVOCATION to specific people, or your family of friends, or your natal family, or your community, your nation, or all of humanity. Its effect will be felt wherever you focus.

Just as with any of the invocations, you begin with THE UNIVERSAL CONNECTION, the simple meditation, for twenty minutes. Then after feeling relaxed and centered, visualize the violet flame whirling around you, expanding to include the whole globe. Wallow in the feeling that you have evoked for awhile. Then think or say the equivalent of the following:

"This invocation is invoked for my benefit and for the benefit of all my friends, past and present, whatever situation, for the benefit of all my natal family, for the benefit of all the people who live in my nation, and for the benefit of all persons everywhere, whatever their ethnicity, race, color, physical characteristics, or nationality. I hereby invoke all the great forces and powers of creation to burn away, transform, change, and correct all inappropriate thoughts, actions, intentions, and emotions, whether known or unknown, that interfere in any way with prosperity, loving relationships, or perfect health. I further invoke the flame to reprogram all subconscious thoughts that interfere with prosperity, loving relationships, or perfect health. From now on the violet flame shall monitor my subconscious thoughts and my outgoing impulses and shall correct them so they are only in accordance with my highest good."

Allow these words to resonate for a few minutes with your eyes closed, as you feel love welling up and the changes taking place.

Of course you need not restrict your invocation to prosperity, health, and relationships. As in all cases with the invocation, you can modify it for specific needs, including tensions and conflicts around the globe.

While anger, meanness, hatred, and hurtful actions of one person does have its effect on all of us, the strength of THE INVOCATION FOR HUMANITY is thousands-fold more powerful. It takes only a few people to change the consciousness of everyone. In physics, scientists call this a phase transition. Only a fraction of order obliterates disorder.

When consciousness is raised, what is the result? For an individual, there is a feeling of love and peace bursting forth. For the society, harmony, caring, and peace is easily maintained. This in essence is the hallmark for people living on the planet Earth for the next millennium. THE INVOCATIONS, using the violet flame and the powers of Almighty Creation, bring this rise in consciousness and maintain it. You now have the means to realize enlightenment for yourself and for peace on earth.

INVOCATION FOR HUMANITY

Begin with twenty minutes or so with THE UNIVERSAL CONNECTION.

Then visualize the violet flame whirling around your whole body and allow it to expand to encompass the whole world.

Think or speak out the equivalent of the following:

"This invocation is invoked for my benefit and for the benefit of all my friends, past and present, whatever situation, for the benefit of all my natal family, for the benefit of all the people who live in my nation, and for the benefit of all persons everywhere, whatever their ethnicity, face, color, physical characteristics, or nationality. I hereby invoke all the great forces and powers of creation to transform, change, and correct all inappropriate thoughts, actions, intentions, and emotions, whether known or unknown, that interfere in any way with prosperity, loving relationships, or perfect health. From now on the violet flame shall monitor my subconscious thoughts and my outgoing impulses and shall correct them so they are only in accordance with my highest good."

Back off and feel love well up as the changes take place.

Part V
Wisdom and Practices

Anything I can do, you can do also, and even greater things thereof.

Jesus

CHAPTER FOURTEEN
Getting Answers

We receive answers about universal truths or your personal life. Using a special technique and within certain guidelines, we simply speak out or think universal truth or personal information that is in our highest and wisest interest to know. It is easy to check the veracity of what you speak out or think, and nothing will ever be received which is harmful to anyone or anything in any way. With practice, answers just appear.

The invocations must seem too simple to be believable. How could such a simple process deliver such profound results?

The power of the violet flame has always been available. However, as mankind sank lower and lower in vibration, the flame slipped from view. It wasn't seen, and there was no access to it. Very recently, as a result of the rising consciousness of a few, mankind's vibration has increased. Now the flame is back in view, and its rewards are easily accessible. It just takes the invocation along with your intent.

In one sense this is new knowledge—at least it appears new. Lost for eons, the return seems like a rebirth. Of course it requires no rebirth because it is the very same as it was at the beginning of creation.

Using the invocations, you erase inappropriate energies that deliver suffering, poverty, and loneliness. There is another gift of the violet flame. You can invoke it to receive truth as it applies in your life, and the truth is as available and abundant as air.

You can ask for knowledge about any subject and receive an answer. Furthermore, you can verify any answer by asking a "yes" or "no" question.

The knowledge that you receive is always only couched in love. The knowledge can not and will never harm anything or anyone, known or unknown. Any information that deviates from this standard is incorrect and a mistake.

The knowledge is also limited to your state of consciousness at this time on this planet. At another time, the knowledge may be different. At another place, it may be different. At different states of your awareness, the knowledge might appear different. Keep this in mind. You can only get information relevant to you. Just because it fits your life is no guarantee it will fit for someone else. It is a very personal procedure.

The practice TAPPING KNOWLEDGE begins with THE UNIVERSAL CONNECTION—that simple meditation—for twenty minutes. When you feel relaxed and centered, visualize the flame, violet in color, whirling around your whole body. Be with that vision for several moments, then ask your question. Back off and be aware of your thoughts. Then speak, or think, the thoughts that come to you. It is a narration, flowing easily. You are not in a trance, but rather just speaking out your thoughts. These are your thoughts because you have access to all knowledge in creation. It is not coming from afar, from another being. You own these thoughts.

They are ordinary, plain, and truthful. During the whole time the movement of your head or torso is to be with you, since this is just a continuation of THE UNIVERSAL CONNECTION.

By invoking the violet flame, you clear the path for your thoughts to tap into the infinite reservoir of knowledge. Only that knowledge which is in your highest and wisest interest to receive will be there.

As you speak out the knowledge, it is only natural to wonder if you're speaking out the knowledge correctly. Well, there is a simple way to find out. Stop the swaying, and with your head carefully balancing on your neck and shoulders, ask, "Am I correctly speaking out truth?" Allow your head freedom to move without trying to move it. Then if the head nods three times, you know you are speaking out the truth. If your head turns either right or left (like a "no" nod), you know you were embellishing and your words were somehow inaccurate.

You ought to practice these "yes" and "no" signals so you're comfortable with them and so you'll be confident you are not forcing the head movements.

Once you feel confident that you can speak out knowledge truthfully, you can also use these "yes" and "no" signals to ask simple questions. You ask a question that has a yes or no answer, and allow the motion of your head to deliver the answer.

Whenever you ask for guidance, always frame your words to elicit only what is in "your highest and wisest interest." These words should be inserted automatically in everything you ask.

Whenever you ask a personal question and get a "no" answer, that "no" answer might be saying you are not going to get an answer to that question. So ask, "Is that a true no?" If not, maybe your question needs to be rephrased, or maybe you should not have the answer at this time. Ask more "yes" and "no" questions to find out the problem.

When you ask a personal question, ask the opposite because it might be in your highest and wisest interest to do something and also not to do it. For instance, it might be in your highest and wisest interest to move to London, and it might also be in your highest and wisest interest not to move to London.

Keep in mind that you will never be able to invade another person's privacy without their permission. You cannot get information about another unless they want you to have it. Any answers about them may not be accurate and cannot be relied upon. Another person's thoughts, intentions, feelings are private by cosmic design. The knowledge you receive can only be that which pertains to you personally.

Most importantly, you will never be given instructions to harm anyone in any way—ever.

Never ask about the future, since we are all constantly making the future. At any moment you or someone else can change that. It is not set in concrete. Whatever you receive will be for the present, and it could very well be different in two months. That means you can't get reliable information on how to invest your money or whom to fall in love with. These imply knowledge for the future.

You may do THE UNIVERSAL CONNECTION with another person and incorporate the request for general knowledge. With someone else, never get into personal questions about either of you. If someone wants such answers, teach that person how to receive it themselves in private.

Questions of a general nature are like this: Are the various kinds of love all the same? Are there other worlds suitable for my home? What happens when I die? Was I created at the time of my conception or before? Do I have a soul? What is my nature beyond the physical body? Am I timeless?

Questions of a personal nature are like this: "Is it in my highest and wisest interest to pursue a career in electronics?" "Is it in my highest and wisest interest to move to London?" "Is it in my highest and wisest interest to open my home to roommates?" Remember, for all personal questions, always ask the opposite? Just because an electronic career is a good move does not mean it is the only good move. For instance ask, "Is it in my highest and wisest interest not to move to London?"

After you have practiced the procedure for tapping into infinite intelligence, you will find that you are always in tune. Answers come with the question. They are just there. That is why this practice plays such a significant role in finding solutions for problems of all kinds, whether global or personal. It is the single most reason to be optimistic for the future.

TAPPING GENERAL KNOWLEDGE

Begin with twenty minutes or so with THE UNIVERSAL CONNECTION.

Then visualize the violet flame whirling around your whole body.

Think or speak out a request to receive universal truth that is appropriate for you to know at this time. You can ask the truth to be on a general subject, or simply be open to whatever truth comes forth.

Allow the movement of your head or torso to continue with THE UNIVERSAL CONNECTION, and speak out the thoughts that come to you.

Periodically ask, "Am I speaking truth?" Look for your head to nod 3 times (meaning yes) or move to the right or left (meaning no).

TAPPING SPECIFIC KNOWLEDGE

Begin with twenty minutes or so with THE UNIVERSAL CONNECTION.

Then visualize the violet flame whirling around your whole body.

Think or speak out a specific question about you personally (and only you), including the words "highest and wisest interest" in every question.

Your head will nod up and down 3 times for a yes answer, and it will sway to either the right or left for a no answer. A "no" answer can also mean the question needs to be rephrased or that you should not know the answer at this time. Ask the opposite question to clarify this "no" answer.

You will never ever be instructed to harm anyone or anything. All answers are only couched in love.

Whatever God's dream about man may be, it seems certain it cannot come true unless man cooperates.

Stella Terrill Mann

CHAPTER FIFTEEN
The Power of Beauty

Since we can trace our Selves to the Unified Field—The Creative Source, where we and everything melts into Oneness, to recognize the beauty in other people, creatures, and things is to behold the beauty in our Selves. To bellow beauty is a high spiritual practice because it connects us to the infinite where there is all power, knowledge, peace, and love.

Our experiences in life are determined by what we see, hear, feel, smell, and taste. If you go to a wonderful restaurant and dwell on what you consider bad service, a small flaw in the food, or even how the smell annoys you, then your experience of this wonderful restaurant is going to be terrible. If you had focused on the beauty that was also there, the whole experience would have been delightful. Beauty is truly in the eyes of the beholder.

Interestingly enough, to experience with all five senses the beauty around us is to experience the beauty in our Selves. To feel our own beauty is to feel the beauty in others. To recognize our own beauty is to salute the beauty in all of creation. This is because we are all one and yet an individual in the cosmos, and to recognize the beauty of a part is to recognize beauty of the whole.

Within us lies all the beauty of the cosmos. We are the Unified Field. We are matter, energy, time, space, and gravity. We are That. When we see our own beauty, and when we voice gratitude for it, we are paying homage to consciousness everywhere. Actually, we are worshiping in the simplest and most meaningful way.

The DNA molecule in our genes carries all the information for our physical existence. It is like a computer that has recorded every bit of knowledge necessary to carry our body from birth to death. It regulates our growth and matures us. It differentiates the organs, senses, and special body parts. It even links us to our species. Biologists marvel at the exactness of the DNA, and each new discovery about it unfolds another layer of its connection to life everywhere.

There is also a COSMIC DNA. It is the "master computer" that stores all information about creation so the body DNA can carry out its function. All information in the COSMIC DNA is for our use and is our link to the entire cosmos. With this linkage we can connect with any other part of the cosmos with the speed of intention and thought. We can and already do this, which is almost unfathomable because we are seemingly locked into space and time constraints.

"If I'm here, you can't be here also" is a law of physics, and it is correct for the physical world on this planet, as far as it goes. However, time, space, and matter all melt into the same at the COSMIC DNA level. There everyone, other beings, and all things share the COSMIC DNA and the Universe and all of Creation with each other.

The COSMIC DNA is infinite in its capacity, and that giant "Master Computer" can let each of us access any part of the cosmos, or Truth, or experience all at once. It is our unrestricted, unfettered link to each other and creation. That is our birthright.

Therefore, to see the beauty in another person is to see the beauty in your own Self. Even to see the beauty in a flower is to see the beauty in your own Self. You and the flower are of the cosmos and hold the entire cosmos within your and its structures, just as a small chip of the hologram contains the entire hologram picture. The flower and your Self are both governed by the same COSMIC DNA. Even though you and the flower are locked into space and time for here and now, both you and the flower exist in the infinite.

This is why seeing the beauty in another person is the same as seeing the same beauty in your Self. Everyone is an expression of that infinite COSMIC DNA, which is the basis of your true Self.

These concepts are both uplifting and baffling. They give us a good feeling, as does all Truth, yet they are as hard to grasp as a cloud. It is not important to figure this out intellectually—not the least bit important. In fact, the awareness we have of the cosmos or metaphysics is not gauged by how well we can write an essay on our infinite connection and the Unified Field. No. Many aware and enlightened people have never heard of these concepts.

The test is rather our perception of beauty. Do we look at a sunset and see beauty? Many people even deprive themselves of taking the time to look. Do we seek those glorious moments around us and marvel at nature's beauty? This is awareness.

Do you see the beauty of a cockroach? A mosquito? A house fly? To love their beauty does not mean we need to enjoy their annoyance, but seeing their beauty is awareness.

When we fall in love, we are really falling in love with our Self. We see the beauty in another person, who sees our beauty and expresses it. Our response is the feeling of being in love. What a gift it is for a loved one to tell us we're beautiful!! The very core of our nature is enlivened. Then, quite naturally the next step is to actually feel our connection to our beloved. This is the first step toward feeling our connection to all that is.

"I feel as though we're never separated." Or, "I've never felt so complete." Or, "We seem to know what each other is thinking." Of course! This is the natural result of being in love, of feeling our own beauty, of being in tune with the infinite. Those phrases are three ways to say the same thing.

We all have people we love, yet how often do we tell someone he or she is beautiful? Too seldom. How often do we tell our friends they're beautiful? Hardly ever. How often do we tell strangers they're beautiful? Never.

If ever we could say "shame on us," it is for failing to see beauty, but shame is not a valid concept. We need not curse our neglect, or place blame, or be shamed. We simply need to turn on the light of beauty now.

Now! Right now, think of someone and say "You're beautiful." At some level he or she can hear you.

You can't think "You're beautiful" too often. Think these words for people passing you on the street. Think

96

them for the butterfly slowly flopping its wings on the long flight south. Think them for the stray dog. Think them for the flower blossom. Let every thought be laced with the beauty around you. You are, of course, merely praising your Self. Yet, without trying to intellectually understand that, you are fully aware of it. You feel it, and you reap the full benefit of knowing it. Besides, this is not something you need to learn. You already have the knowledge; it's built into the COSMIC DNA, the basis of who we are.

If you have a lover, or live with someone, let "Good morning, beautiful" be the first words each day to him or her. Your relationship will bloom. Your day will prosper. With a little tenacity and practice, it will become second nature, and the joys of the experience will quickly overshadow that bashfulness.

"Beautiful" is a very powerful word. However, we can use lots of expressions and synonyms to say the same thing. "You have a special sparkle today." "Your eyes are shining." "You're stunning." "You're quite handsome, you know." "You're very pretty."

At the checkout line in the supermarket, don't be afraid to tell the woman next to you her hairdo is gorgeous. Don't be afraid to notice a beautiful shirt, or any other article of clothing that was obviously carefully chosen. Whenever you approach someone, however, be certain the compliment is unconditional, quick, and non-invasive. If your compliment is given for a purpose, it loses its punch. You want it to be an unconditional recognition of someone's beauty.

Speaking out beauty can be called THE BEAUTIFUL BEATITUDE. In time this will be the outward hallmark of spiritual people. We will be extolling the beauty of everyone and everything around us. In recognizing beauty to one small segment of creation, we recognize the beauty in everyone, in all of Nature, in the entire Universe, and to our Selves. Above all, we will be enlivening our awareness.

We can't see beauty without broadening our awareness. Our vision is awakened in so many ways with this experience. As a man thinks, so he is. Think beauty, and your experience becomes beauty. Think beauty, and you radiate beauty for everyone. Think beauty, and your heart opens to touch the infinite. In your mind the infinite may remain a hazy abstraction, but in your heart, the infinite will paint the feelings of joy, and bliss, and happiness. This is our gift to ourselves by simply saying "You're beautiful" to someone.

THE BEAUTIFUL BEATITUDE

Bellow beauty with these four new habits:

Say "Good morning, beautiful" or the equivalent to the first person you see each day.

Think "You're beautiful" for all life forms.

Think "You're beautiful" for strangers that pass by you.

Say the equivalent of "You're beautiful" with compliments to everyone as often as possible.

When you think or say "You're beautiful" or the equivalent, feel that you are affirming your own beauty because we are all one. Know also that your thoughts and words of beauty return to grace your own experiences.

PART V   Wisdom for Living

And your very flesh shall be a great poem
Walt Whitman

CHAPTER SIXTEEN
Body Beautiful

Our physical bodies are made up of millions of individual cells and organs, all aware of our attitude toward them. By giving love to our bodies, we gain maximum enjoyment from them. We can give love by stating it and by running our hands all over our bodies, showing love, appreciation, and awe. Our bodies tie us to the here and now, and they must be appreciated and loved to support our lives.

What we think, every cell in our body hears. That is so important to realize. If you hate your body, every cell will know and react in disappointment.

So many people want their body to be different from what it is. Too large, too small, too thin, too thick, too tall, too short, wrong color. The energy and thought people give to hating their body is astonishing.

These disapproving thoughts are not secret. They hit our bodies like a stick hits a drum. Each cell is bathed in the reverberating thought, "I hate you, I hate you."

What kind of results would the president of a large corporation get by constantly voicing dissatisfaction, hate, or disgust for the employees? By the same token, what kind of productivity would be achieved by appreciating and praising them? These are obvious rhetorical questions, and it is the same with our bodies.

Each cell, grouped into departments called organs, responds the same way.

Your body functions like a mini-Universe. There are billions of cells. Each one is alive with consciousness. Think about this. Your body is not just you, but rather it is a collection of bodies for billions of other creatures that are conscious and aware.

Each cell relates to its environment, as we do, or as planet earth relates to the solar system or milky way. Each cell is specialized, and each cell has the intelligence needed to know how and what to do. It knows the nutrients, minerals, salts, electrolytes, water, or oxygen it needs, and then pulls them out of its environment. If the material isn't there, it improvises as best it can.

The cells are clustered together into organs and body parts, each with a particular function. Each of these parts also has consciousness, as indeed does all life. We humans are so egotistical that we often think that we have a monopoly on consciousness, awareness, and feelings. That's not the case. Our bodies are comprised of an entire creation of conscious beings, each with a purpose and a desire to serve. They range from the cell, to the individual organs, to the whole body. Each is a life form that exists in its own right.

We are not just our physical bodies. Temporarily we use it to anchor ourselves into this time on planet earth. We each have our own immutable permanent body of other layers and vibrations. The physical body is easiest to identify with and controls so much of our quality of life.

Every being responds to its environment. We are no exception. When we're working for people who don't like us, we do sloppy work, give up, become depressed, or quit. It is the same with each cell. It does its work best when it is surrounded by praise and the feelings of love.

The "I hate you" thought does vibrate throughout the body. It is picked up, heard, and felt by every single cell and organ we so desperately need to enjoy life. Likewise, the "I love you" thought bathes them to produce an entirely different atmosphere.

A loving home for a child is the greatest gift parents can give. In the business world, an appreciation of workers is one of the secrets to increase productivity. We have ignored those same principles for our beautiful body. Now is the time to turn this around with a special kind of spiritual experience, BODY BEAUTIFUL. This is so simple it might seem a waste of energy.

BODY BEAUTIFUL is simply relating to the physical body your feelings of love for it. Run your hands all over your body while saying "I love you," or "I am grateful to you," or "You're beautiful." The exact words are not important. You need only convey love and appreciation for the physical body you now inhabit.

A wonderful way to unify with your body is to incorporate THE LOVE CONNECTION. While running your hands all over your body, say to it, "I give you my love, I give you my heart, I receive your love, I receive your heart." Or you can think these three sentences: "I give every cell in my body love and gratitude. I give every organ in my body love and gratitude. I give my whole body love and gratitude."

We label it "polite" to praise someone else's body. We say we're "conceited" to praise our own. Nonsense! Praising and loving your body is no less than good management. You have billions of little beings working in your "factory." Be a good manager. Praise and love them privately. Praise and love them publicly. They do respond.

This does not mean we don't get rid of extra pounds, if indeed they are more than just a body type. We always do what we can from our side to have a gorgeous, healthy body. The point is we never stop loving it in the process. We actively send the love and gratitude it deserves.

We need to do everything in our power to give our bodies maximum working conditions. Any good manager would do that. For instance, exercise regularly. After all, you take your dog for a daily walk. Do the same for your body. Find the kind of routine both you and your body will enjoy. Then make a pact to exercise regularly.

Eat correctly. This is different for everyone, and seems to change periodically as well. There are common sense guidelines, however. Fresh food is preferred whenever possible. Try to avoid additives, even those added to the feed of beef or poultry. Neither starve yourself, nor overeat. Greasy, salty, sugary, junk foods are usually just that—junk.

Eliminate recreation drugs, whether eaten, smoked, or mainlined. Besides destroying cells, they cut right into our ability to experience THE UNIVERSAL CONNECTION.

Sleep at regular intervals and for the amount of time your body needs. During the day have periods of rest, including some form of meditation such as THE UNIVERSAL CONNECTION.

Every person's body is a unique creation. There are no hard and fast rules that can apply for everyone. Fortunately, we need not guess. We can ask our bodies what they need or want. Using the same procedure for getting answers, simply ask you body. With the aid of "yes" and "no" signals, your body will talk to you. We can locate and strengthen the conscious bond we already have with our bodies.

Call this THE BODY BOND. You will become close friends with your body. You will develop total trust in each other, and like an effective marriage, you will communicate openly. Bonding regularly with your body and actively responding to its physical needs is the first step toward perfect health. That is the gift from a body that's loved and listened to.

BODY BEAUTIFUL

Run your hands all over your body while thinking:

I give every cell in my body love and gratitude.

I give every organ in my body love and gratitude.

I give my whole body love and gratitude.

THE BODY BOND

Begin with twenty minutes or so with THE UNIVERSAL CONNECTION.

Then visualize the violet flame whirling around your whole body.

Ask you body if there is something you are doing that you need to stop or something that it specifically needs. Listen and speak out the answer.

Using the technique for getting answers (Chapter 14), periodically check that you are speaking truth. Let your head nod three times for "yes" and move to right or left for a "no".

Chapter Seventeen
Affection and Sex

*Affection and sex are a path for enlightenment—
connecting us to the Unified Field. At every
opportunity, we need to show affection to everyone we
meet in an inoffensive way, even silently. Follow basic
guidelines for making love an integral part of every
sexual experience by giving and receiving love and by
bellowing beauty. We can easily learn about our own
sexual needs, while being without judgment concerning
other people's needs and orientation.*

Whatever you put out will boomerang back many fold. Voice beauty, and you'll hear how beautiful you are. Give someone a loving gesture, and you'll be showered with affection in return. This is simply a fundamental law of nature.

Giving universal love is extremely important for developing loving unions. Don't be afraid to touch in any way not offensive to the other person. Such demonstration need not be restricted to people in love, but friends of all kinds can show it.

That gentle tug, that squeeze of the hand, that wink, that smile, that pat on the back—these are all possible in public without offending anyone. These are signals that we care, and with them we open up the channel even wider for the perfect mate to flow into and remain in our life.

The inoffensive public gesture of love is not a full blown open mouth kiss. It isn't sexually explicit, or even implicit. It is only a simple love acknowledgement. More than likely, the gesture will be unnoticed, but the emotion and Truth of love will give it power to rock creation, cleanse mass-consciousness, and return to us in the form of rewarding relationships.

Encourage a display of affection between all people in your home, in front of children, and in front of strangers. There is nothing to fear with this. Instead it is the lack of affection we need to fear. The person who is unable to touch is destined for loneliness.

Of course, affection is not sex. That is precisely why it can be so powerful. To give affection unconditionally without sexual prowess is the highest gift of the heart.

That is not to diminish the importance of sex in your relationship. Sex is undeniably a significant part of our lives. Our choice of friends, our close relationships, our choice of careers, our choice of abodes, our choice of cities, our recreation, our spirituality—all these and more are a product of our sexuality. In every case, sex has compelled us into specific directions, and a specific life-style. It has all been for maximum good in the long haul. When that finally dawns, none of us could possibly want to be anyone else, or even to be ourselves with a different set of traits and qualities. We are perfectly equipped now for what we came to accomplish.

Total acceptance of our sexuality is a giant step in Self-acceptance. Accepting that we are a unique expression of the Almighty Cosmos right now, yet at the same time that we are infinitely everything, is the grand realization. Everyone is sexually unique, and that is the backdrop for Self-acceptance.

There are many, many ideas on sex, and it seems that many are denials of it. Even the practices linked to spiritual disciplines seem to inhibit full sexual expression. These various rules and practices do have their place for some people. They do not, however, have universal application. Instead we need a set of simple guidelines so that our spirituality and our sexuality augment each other and aren't at cross purposes.

Such guidelines would include non-judgment. We must be without judgment. We must accept everyone as unique and perfect, free to find and to express sex in any way he or she feels comfortable. We do this without thinking how strange, even in our private-most thoughts. We don't snicker, shun, or condemn any form of sexual expression so long as it doesn't interfere with or do harm to others.

Another guideline for sex would be to always strive to feel THE LOVE CONNECTION. It may not always be there, but go into the act with that in mind. Whether a one night stand, a lover, or a spouse, let your awareness be with the feelings of love that can bubble up. Focus on them. They're your feelings, of course, but the sex act is the catalyst for them. Afterward, lie quietly together and let those feelings gel. Sex can truly be a love connection, but it will require your intention and focus.

By lying together in an embrace, you set up the perfect time to think, "I give you my love, I give you my heart, I receive your love, I receive your heart." Then wallow in the feelings of being unified together. Feel them well up, and well up they will.

109

Remember THE BEAUTIFUL BEATITUDE. Let it become an integral part of sex. Whisper the beauty of your lover and your love-making experience.

THE UNIVERSAL CONNECTION also plays a role here. When we connect to the Unified Field, that most elementary vibration that underlies everything, we have a feeling of love. That is actually what creation feels like, and our nervous system is capable of picking it up and experiencing it. It is experienced as love. So when your sex emphasizes and brings out feelings of love, you are actually feeling the Unified Field. We can make a conscious effort to cultivate those feelings of love with sex. At the same time we can use sex to unify with all of creation by recognizing our own and our partner's beautiful qualities. Know and feel these qualifies when you're having sex.

Guidance on what is your best sexual expression and even your "partner's best" is always available with the practice called TAPPING KNOWLEDGE. This is your best ally in knowing everything you want and need to know about sex. After all, you can't read a book written by someone else on everything you need to know now about your sex life. No-one else can tell you what that is for you, but the answers are for the asking.

The hallmark of sex is that it is very simple, and we need not complicate it. These basic guidelines help to keep it simple, while emphasizing the love it is meant to bring into our lives.

However you choose to express sex, know it is your choice and not a mistake of nature. Know your sexual orientation is only for good. At the same time be without judgment about the many legitimate ways other people express sex. We are all unique expressions of the

110

infinite, and how each of us expresses the infinite contributes to the beautiful collage of life: unity in diversity—diversity in unity.

PUBLIC AFFECTION

When you are with a friend or someone you love, give that person an inoffensive touch signifying your connection. The circumstances dictate the appropriateness. At an airport, a long hug and a light kiss might be right. At the Ritz, perhaps only a squeeze on the arm is comfortable. These are not just for public display, but primarily for us to show genuine thoughts of public love without fear, so they will bounce back to influence our lives.

GUIDELINES FOR SEX

Be without judgment concerning other people's sexual orientation and expression.

In your thoughts whisper to your partner THE LOVE CONNECTION.

Acknowledge your partner's beauty.

Know and feel the power of a sexual union in bringing your conscious awareness to the Unified Field — the feeling of love.

Learn more about your sexual needs with the practice of TAPPING KNOWLEDGE.

CHAPTER EIGHTEEN
Love As The Unified Field

*Love is the Unified Field, so it is the most fundamental
vibration from which everything in creation arises.
Simply by connecting to that innermost source, we can
feel love and experience everyone and everything as
One. To harm any aspect of creation is to harm our
own Selves. When we give and receive love we elevate
everyone on the planet to some degree to experience
that Oneness. The effect we all have on each other is
enormous.*

We start with the basic Truth we now know about
love: it is The Creative Source, the Unified Field, the
most elementary aspect in creation. Everything and
everyone is made of love, and all of creation is love.
Nature is simply different expressions of that same basic
love energy, and we are capable of experiencing and
feeling that most subtle aspect of creation.

All of humankind's creations are also love—our
buildings, cars, clothes, factories, even chemicals, guns,
and bombs. Nothing can exist that is not from that basic
elementary energy—The Unified Field.

Our physical DNA is made of love. The cosmic
DNA is also love. Love is the slippery thread that
connects all of us with every other being in creation.

Even more remarkable than this very simple
understanding of a complex creation is that you are

made to feel that love. What this means is that you are able to tune into your true nature. As observer you discover you are also the observed. What you actually observe is that everything is an aspect of your "Self". This is because whatever you observe has that same basic indivisible energy of love for its building block as you do.

You can literally observe another person and say, "I am that." Or you can look at a tree and say, "I am that." Or you can marvel at a tide pool and think, "I am that." Or you can gaze into the night sky and whisper, "I am that."

The realization that we are love and that everything else is also love personalizes the impersonal world. We never intentionally would hurt our own Selves—at least not without a distorted outlook. So, is it a distorted outlook to kill whole species of animals for sport or reckless harvesting, to send acid and smog into our air, to pour chemicals into our rivers and lakes, or kill each other in the name of religion, or territory, or money? Of course it is because in reality we are inflicting self wounds.

We can't put filth into our world without putting filth into our own Selves, because we share the soul of love with all that is around us. We can't hurt another human without it being self infliction. All the cries of nature, the screams of slain soldiers, the yelping of tortured animals reverberate throughout the cosmos, just as the singing of a whale or group of whales can be heard in the sea around the world.

We are in a sea of love. We are individual expressions within that sea, but the sea is our foundation. Whatever we do to the foundation will surely affect the structure of our life.

When we all realize WE ARE THAT, then we will quickly stop all this Self infliction. This is our goal as enlightened people.

All of nature constantly tries to right what humankind has wronged. We deforest a range, and nature tries to grow it back. We foul the air, and nature tries to purge and clean. We wound another person's flesh, and nature tries to heal. We constantly marvel at the power of nature and her persistence in bringing back balance, regardless of our continuing assaults upon her. This is the power of love.

The power of love is so great that only a small amount of it neutralizes tons of negative influence. This is the power of a group doing THE LOVE CONNECTION together. Only a few people coming together for this purpose can raise the consciousness of everyone. In this simple practice as a group, balance on the planet can be gained and maintained. That, of course, was the purpose of the cloisters of holy people throughout the ages. Now the effect can be even more powerful.

The group practicing THE LOVE CONNECTION has its effect because we are all one love, The Creative Source, the Unified Field. Being connected, we forever change to some degree what everyone perceives. Eventually, we all perceive ourselves as love, as connected, as whole, and as One. And it all happens as a whisper, everyone realizing ah-ha experiences.

115

THE GROUP LOVE CONNECTION

The group leader asks each member to close their eyes and meditate in their own way.

The group leader then asks each member to think of a particular national leader and then recites each of the four sentences to be focused on that leader, pausing after each sentence: "I give you my love; I give you my heart; I accept your love; I accept your heart."

The group leader can go through any number of specific names in like manner, reciting the four sentences to be focused on each person.

The group leader then tells each person to think of a special person in their life, then reciting the four sentences to be focused on each person.

CHAPTER NINETEEN
Forgiveness

Life is "for giving" love. "Forgiving" love. Forgiving is just recognizing that life is "for giving" love, and that you forgive by giving love. To hold a grudge gives power to the illusion that someone else can hurt us. We neither need tell the person we forgive, nor forget anything. Just send love in any number of creative ways.

Forgiveness is misunderstood. To understand forgiveness, just remember that all of creation is made of love, and we are made to receive that love. That is what life is for: to receive creation's love. However, life isn't just for receiving love. Life is also for giving love to everyone and everything.

This little Truth unlocks easy forgiving. Life is for giving love. "For giving." "For giving" love. That is forgiveness. It's just giving love. Nothing more.

When we hold grudges, we are choosing to withhold that sweet taste of love we can give. Get rid of that grudge, and once again your life is "for giving" love.

Grudges are really easy to release once we realize what a silly illusion they are. We hold grudges because we think someone has hurt us. We imagine we have been trespassed, compromised, attacked, or in some

117

way made a lesser person. Such folly! We are perfection, and no one can alter that.

"You have done me wrong, but I don't want to hold a grudge, so I am going to try to forget that terrible thing you did." What is wrong with those words? They recognize an illusion. They give power to a mistake: that anyone could harm us without our consent. It is impossible. We are creators, and no one can interfere with our creation without our consent, even though we may not be hearing that consent. Our own creation begins with our thoughts and we must take responsibility for what we think.

So instead of trying to place blame as part of forgiving, the correct formula is simply to give love. For instance, think these words:

"I have made a mistake in my thinking to allow you to seemingly hurt me. I recognize that you are merely doing what I invited, and that in reality neither you nor anyone else can hurt me. I am perfect now, always have been, and always will be, and nothing can change that. I now recognize that life is for giving love and I give love to you."

An abbreviated version of these forgiving words can be:

"I send you love from my heart, and I forgive you, knowing it is impossible for you to infringe on my perfection."

In this technique of forgiveness, don't restrict yourselves by giving love to just those who bother you. Also give love to those you truly do love, often and

118

unsolicited. You can do this by thinking "I send you love from my heart."

Forgiveness is a marvelous way to go to sleep at night. Our thoughts before sleep can improve our rest and mental processing, and of course thoughts of love carry the highest and purest vibration. Before going to sleep, just think of people that flash into your awareness and think "I give you my love."

Giving love changes the consciousness of the receiver. You can't put honey on a person's tongue and not have it tasted. When you send love energy, it actually permeates your recipients, whether or not they are aware of it. With it comes a degree of insight, peace, vitality, and optimism. One infusion won't change their world completely, but it does make a difference, and it builds up, automatically, without confrontation or explanation.

THE LOVE CONNECTION—those four sentences of giving and receiving love and heart—is another form of forgiveness. You can use it instead of these other suggestions, or you can dream up one of your very own. The only important point is that giving love alone is the act of forgiveness. Nothing else needs to be thought. You don't need to recreate or harp on any situation. You don't need to communicate your forgiveness to the other person. And you don't need to forget either. You simply give love. And when you do, all tensions spontaneously cease. If the tensions return, again give love.

A corollary to this technique is to randomly give love to people who pass by you. You do this silently to friends, strangers, fellow workers, or whomsoever you're around. This is such a simple thing, and one day all of mankind will understand its power and significance.

In this way we can change the world. We just need to remember that life is for giving love, and then to give love to those who bother us and to those we truly do love.

THE FORGIVENESS FORMULA

Recognize that life is "for giving" love and then generously give that love. As often as the urge comes, silently say to those around you or those you visualize (regardless of your relationship to them):

"My life is for giving love. Thus, I give you love from my heart."

If there is some roughness between you and anyone, think the essence of these words as you give love:

"I have made a mistake in my thinking to allow you to seemingly hurt me. I recognize that you are merely doing what I invited, and that in reality neither you nor anyone else can hurt me. I am perfect now, always have been, and always will be. You can't change that. I now recognize that life is for giving love to you, so I now give you love from my heart."

What the superior man seeks is in himself; what the small man seeks is in others.

Confucius

CHAPTER TWENTY
Relationships

*Relationships form whenever people come together,
whether two or thousands. It is a separate energy with
consciousness, and it is the sum total of the people who
make it up. We can get guidance from the relationships
about what they need, and we can empower the ones
we want. Understanding the nature of relationships
changes every aspect of our lives, since relationships
are intricately a part of everything we are and do.*

Relationship between any two people is actually an energy. It matters not if it's between two men, two women, or a man and a woman. It matters not their sexual involvement. The phenomenon is the same. All the gross and subtle energies of one person are combined with those of the other. The sum total is the relationship. The energies are not added together, so as to augment and cancel each other like sound, electricity, or light. Instead, all the energies of the two people are present in this new bundle of energy. It actually does exist, and when science becomes more sophisticated, the relationship will be located and measured.

Furthermore this new bundle of energy we call a relationship has intelligence and consciousness. You can be guided by the intelligence of your relationships.

Without help, it is unlikely you would know what is best for the relationship. You can't know that because you don't know the other person's energies and needs, or how they mesh with yours. That's why in the scheme of nature, a whole separate, intelligent, and conscious energy is born when two people come together. You are intimately connected to that relationship energy, and it can be a guiding light if you open yourself to it.

This phenomena isn't limited to lover relationships. Every conceivable type and size of relationship has this energy and consciousness: you and your parents, you and friends, you and your siblings, your whole family, your whole household, your class at school, your support group, your city, your ethnic group, your countrymen, and everyone on earth.

Blending together of souls is called "Mass-consciousness". It is an energy made up of all the people in a group, whether two or thousands. That consciousness contains all the knowledge about everyone in that group. It holds their ideas and aspirations, and it contains all their beliefs. It also knows Truth, and it can nudge and guide the group. What we experience with a lover, we also experience as a nation. There is a relationship—a mass-consciousness—for each and every conceivable combination. The immensity of the relationship energies is staggering, but nature is infinite, and there are no boundaries. There's plenty of room for all these combinations.

When you realize your relationship is actually energy, it is very exciting. It then makes sense to say "our relationship needs...," or "our relationship is...," or "it's in the highest and wisest interest of our relationship that...." You say this because your relationship has life, has energy, has intelligence, and has consciousness. Your relationship knows what is best for it and for each of you.

You can communicate with the relationship with the practice of TAPPING KNOWLEDGE. The procedure is the same. Begin with twenty minutes or so of THE UNIVERSAL CONNECTION. Then visualize the violet flame engulfing you and others in the relationship. Be with that vision until you feel connected. Then employ the same techniques for asking questions. If two or more people understand and practice TAPPING KNOW-LEDGE, they can do this together, speaking aloud the questions and answers.

Using this tool we can quickly learn all about our various relationships. Furthermore, we can empower whichever ones we want by our mere intention. That's important to understand. We are not victims or slaves to these energy fields called relationships. We decide which ones are to be dominant. The decision doesn't even need to be conscious. It's a matter of focus or intention. Knowing they exist and that we can empower them is the first step in gaining greater control over our lives. Since we live with and amongst other people, we can choose which of our relationships to empower and emphasize. That empowerment is from your perspective, since you cannot interfere with another person's relationships or their priorities. When all members of the relationship decide to empower with their desire and intention (whether expressed or not), the relationship takes on special and dynamic force.

By carefully monitoring our principle relationships, we can improve their quality. We empower the ones we want, then we learn how to make them more fulfilling and successful for everyone, easily and without guessing.

THE RELATIONSHIP CONNECTION

Begin with twenty minutes or so with THE UNIVERSAL CONNECTION.

Then visualize the violet flame whirling around everyone in the relationship.

Think or speak out a request to receive universal truth that is appropriate for you to know at this time about the relationship. You can ask the truth to be on a general subject, or simply be open to whatever truth comes forth.

Allow the movement of your head or torso to continue with THE UNIVERSAL CONNECTION, and speak out the thoughts that come to you.

Periodically ask, "Am I speaking truth?" Look for your head to nod 3 times (meaning yes) or move to the right or left (meaning no).

Think or speak out a specific question about the relationship, including the words "highest and wisest interest" in every question.

Your head will nod up and down 3 times for a yes answer, and it will sway to either the right or left for a no answer. A "no" answer can also mean the question needs to be rephrased or that you should not know the answer at this time. Ask another question to clarify this "no" answer.

You will never ever be instructed to harm anyone or anything. The source of all answers is love.

CHAPTER TWENTY-ONE
Mass-Consciousness

For every group there is a mass-consciousness — the beliefs of the group. Since we are one with the group, we can change the thinking of a group by changing our own. Even more powerful is the concerted desire of a few to change the thinking in a group. All thoughts in tune with the laws of nature are so powerful, it only takes a few people to have a profound effect on mass-consciousness. That holds whether the group is small or the entire human race.

We are all subject to the attitudes of our outside world. Too thin. Too fat. Too feminine. Too masculine. Uneducated. Too hairy. Disabled. Too short. Too tall. Gay. Transsexual. Airhead. Blond. Bald. Old. Juvenile. And on and on and on.

Each label conjures up an image that most likely does not come from personal experience. It is part of the "mass-consciousness" that comes from one or more of our relationships. On a grand scale, mass-consciousness is the sum total of all our thoughts and attitudes as a society. Each of us wallows in that mass-consciousness, and we can't escape it, though we can disavow the aspects that foster erroneous beliefs. You have the power to change your own thoughts when you realize you're harboring erroneous and unfounded notions. That is always your prerogative. You'll still be aware of the mass-consciousness, but it will have no hold on you.

127

Furthermore, your single thought is more powerful than you imagine. An ounce of Truth corrects tons of untruth because nature constantly strives to correct imbalance. Until all the errors in mass-consciousness are corrected, the roadblocks against an easy, successful and happy life can seem insurmountable.

Even though one person correcting erroneous beliefs has great effects, the greatest power to correct mass-consciousness lies with groups. The power of a group thinking a single Truth together under one roof is found by squaring the number of people. Only fifteen people thinking Truth together would have the power of 225 thinking Truth alone. Sixteen is the same as 256, to show what happens with even one more.

Because of the power of a group, the practice called THE MASS-CONSCIOUSNESS CORRECTION is for groups, and of course it is simple. Come up with about five Truths that you want to infuse into the mass-mind. Don't be concerned about the misconceptions your Truth needs to correct. We don't have to address them at all. Just dwell on the Truth. You can use the same Truths at each meeting, or you can compile a different list each time. If by chance an untruth creeps onto a list, don't worry. The tremendous power of groups is really only effective for Truth. False notions don't have the support of the cosmos and require far more people to have any effect.

As an example, a list of Truths might look like this:

"Everyone in all races is created with all of the same innate qualities."

"Forgiveness is accomplished by giving love."

"When humanity assaults nature with pollution, we are assaulting our own Self."

"Abundance is my birthright."

"All people are divinely holy, regardless of their race, national original, sexual orientation, size, handicaps, attitudes, or whatever."

When the list is agreed upon, the leader tells everyone to close their eyes with THE UNIVERSAL CONNECTION. Soft harmonic music is optional for this to continue for twenty minutes or so. Then the leader tells everyone to visualize a violet flame engulfing and encircling the entire society holding erroneous beliefs. With everyone holding that vision, the leader speaks out the first Truth on the list, followed by a minute of silence. The leader then tells the group to think that same Truth, followed by another minute of silence.

Each of the Truths on the list is thought in this manner: two impulses, one aloud, one silent, each followed by a minute of silence.

You are part of humanity. You add to the sum total of mass-consciousness. This isn't a role you can accept or reject. If you want to keep buying into erroneous stereotyped thinking, that is what you'll be reinforcing. If you want to change it, you can. There is no excuse for it to be so full of misinformation. You can help fill that mass-consciousness with Truth.

All of us would like to be broad minded and accept other people's ideas. That's all fine, but the fact is there are mountains of false beliefs. Many of these false beliefs

129

are interfering with our lives, so we have a personal incentive to change them.

Truth is not a variable. It just is. You don't need to feel pompous to know it because it is available for everyone. Furthermore, you don't ever have to guess what is Truth. You can easily learn it by the practice of TAPPING KNOWLEDGE. The answers learned in that way are Truth. Always verify a truth using this practice.

Truths are statements about love, the Unified Field. Truths express the order of creation. They are, therefore, at the fundamental fiber of nature. The mere utterance of such a basic concept sends thrills throughout all of creation, especially through the sea of mass-consciousness. When the vibration of Truth echoes in mass-consciousness, it does so with such fury as to shatter anything out of tune with it—like the singer's high C shatters a goblet.

Untruth does not have this shattering ability. It's like a weak note that leaves only a small imprint. The shrill of Truth shatters. Even one of us thinking Truth regularly shatters, to some degree, the untruth of mass-consciousness. Don't underestimate your own power of thinking alone. It is tremendous because of the nature of Truth. Thinking in a group is like exploding a hydrogen bomb, and thinking alone is like exploding an atomic bomb. Both are powerful weapons for changing the world.

This is why our thoughts are so very important. We are rearranging mass-consciousness. We must be aware constantly of what we think. This can't be over-emphasized. Monitor your thoughts, not just because they come back with greater intensity, but because they influence mass-consciousness.

Everyone appears to have huge antennas hundreds of feet tall scanning the airwaves. These are both transmitters and receivers. By our thoughts we send out messages of what we expect, believe, want, fear, or long for. Other people pick these up, and if they jibe with their own expectations, beliefs, desires, fears, or longings, they come to us to "help out." It's all perfect. Everyone is helping everyone else get what they broadcast they want. That is precisely why it is so very important to think correctly and to change mass-consciousness if you want a fulfilling life.

If we find ourselves thinking something inappropriate or something we don't want to experience, it is very easy to erase. We just think, along with the feeling and emotion that accompanies the correct thought: "That's not correct. I cancel that." And it is done. From time to time we all have fear thoughts, or anger, or other inappropriate ideas that can be the foundation for our world tomorrow. We have them because they are floating around in mass-consciousness. When they come up, we can simply take note, disclaim them, and correct our thinking and feelings

MASS-CONSCIOUSNESS CORRECTION
A Group Procedure

Compile a list of five affirmative Truths (as verified with the practice Tapping Specific Knowledge in Chapter 14) for a group to think together at the same time under one roof. The group is then led through this meditation-like experience.

LEADER: "Close your eyes and get centered and relaxed. Connect your breathing so there is no space between the in and out breaths. If you feel your head or torso swaying, breath normally and allow your attention to be with that." (20 minutes or so)

LEADER: "Visualize a flame, violet in color, whirling around and through everyone in our group (define)." (a few moments)

LEADER: "Continue to visualize the violet flame while I read the first Truth from our list."----Reads first Truth. (One minute of silence)

LEADER: "Now think once again that Truth." (One minute of silence)

Continue in this manner for about five separate affirmative Truths.

CHAPTER TWENTY-TWO
Conquering Fear

Whether fear is a general unfocused condition or focused on something, if it has no rational purpose, it can be very debilitating. We can get rid of those fears by identifying them with certainty and by erasing them.

Beliefs are the foundation for what we think. Some beliefs are related to beliefs society holds, and others are beliefs more personal to you. Those that are false we know how to correct.

The formula seems simple. Watch your thoughts, correct the ones that are inappropriate, and then manifest your desires. It should be that simple.

"I didn't want to fail in my business," you say, "but I did." Or, "I work my fingers to the bone, and I still can't get ahead." You may even try affirmations that you repeat each morning, post on the car dash, or record to hear again and again. Yet, your experience isn't what you say you want.

The simple fact long recognized by educators, psychologists, and scientists is that our many subconscious beliefs supersede and overpower our conscious desires. That is their role. At some point we deem certain beliefs so important we give them an "automatic status." Whatever else we are to think, we

133

decree that the certain beliefs we place into our subconscious will automatically guide our lives.

You put the beliefs into your subconscious mind, although the procedure isn't understood and you seldom know you're doing it. For instance, if you experienced or perceived any kind of pain with wealth, or if you were taught that wealth was somehow unholy, bad, immoral, or corrupting, you may have programmed "I want to avoid money." This belief, once programmed into your subconscious mind, will stay there until you clearly intend to remove it.

Sometimes the beliefs in our subconscious mind are beliefs from mass-consciousness—what everyone seems to believe. These beliefs are all around us. We hear them without even being aware of them. We intuitively know what they are, and they are so powerful that we opt to accept these without question. In computer language, they are our "default setting." We hold these beliefs without question, without examining their basis, without realizing they are there, and without knowing how they affect our lives.

In order to change that subconscious program you need to intend to change it. INTENTION is the key.

Before you can intend to do anything, you have to know precisely what it is you do intend. It is very difficult to change a belief you've put into the subconscious until you know what that belief is, why you intend to replace it, and what new belief you intend to replace it with. That is why affirmations often fail. The false belief remains because you signaled no clear intention to remove it.

THE INVOCATIONS automatically reprogram your beliefs, conscious and subconscious, that could interfere with your health, your prosperity, your relationships, and all other aspects of your life. The procedure is simple and direct. On the issue of wealth, natural law provides for wealth and abundance for everyone. Anything less results from faulty thinking that inhibits the natural flow of wealth. When you have thoughts that allow you to accept the flow, money will come. It is just a matter of being in tune with the flow of nature's energy—the same energy that fires the sun, that transforms a seed into an oak tree, and that gives each of us the experience of being alive. You are created with all it takes to experience nature's energy to the fullest. Money and all other forms of abundance are aspects of that natural energy.

Besides from the thoughts that are cleaned up with THE INVOCATIONS, there is another great inhibitor that keeps the good life at bar. It is the insidious, all-pervasive, and debilitating fear.

Feelings of fear come about when you don't perceive the whole picture. Fear requires some lack of knowledge. There is such perfect order in the Universe that you could never be afraid if you knew everything. That idea may be contrary to your understanding.

Because of our limited perception, fear is sometimes inevitable. If we run into a lion on a mountain trail and death appears imminent, we would no doubt experience fear. However, if we knew how we fit into the whole scheme of life, what happens with and after death, what our role on earth is and why it may be coming to an end—if we indeed saw the whole picture, we couldn't be afraid.

135

That is not where most of us are at. We don't know everything. There are going to be times when we are frightened for good reasons, and we'll act as best we can. When a lion appears, we'll fight or flee because we are correctly afraid. That kind of fear is life supporting. However, most fears come from imagined dangers. Such fears need to be managed with wisdom.

A general state of worry is one such fear that interferes with your ability to manifest wealth, health, love, or whatever. Worry thoughts are incredibly powerful. They carry such a wallop that too often you manifest what you are most afraid of. If you're worried you won't have enough money to pay your bills, chances are you won't. If you are worried you won't get a certain job, or promotion, or raise, you probably won't. If you are worried you're going to run out of money, you probably will. It is that simple, folks. If you dwell on anything with enough worry, I guarantee you'll get something pretty close to it.

We're going to tackle two kinds of fear. First, we'll deal with the general condition of fear. Second, we'll tackle fear you associate with specific sets of circumstances. The techniques to come to grips with these fears will break down more walls separating you from your wealth, health, love, and all other aspects of the good life.

Have you awakened at night worried? Or have you worn a frown all day? Often you'll justify your worry. You'll find something to focus on, but as soon as that gets resolved, you'll find something else to worry about. This general worried state is quite crippling. It will surely affect your experiences, and might even help bring about what you are afraid of. As soon as possible you need to break out of it. Don't linger or wallow, because it is very powerful.

There are a few first aid tips for helping a person snap out of the worry state, though it is temporary. The objective is to breathe fast and deep so you take in a lot of oxygen. The general state of worry has a physiological component that is transformed with deep breathing. Do whatever is comfortable to get your breath moving. Run or walk fast. Do pushups, sit-ups, or other kinds of body exercise. You'll be amazed what it does for your frame of mind. Of course, use common sense, and don't push your body beyond comfortable limits. Always follow the advice of your physician when exercising.

The second technique also deals with breath. Sit comfortably and place your right thumb over your right nostril (or left if you're left handed). Breath in deeply, then out. Then move your middle finger over the opposite nostril, breath in deeply, then out. Repeat for several minutes, and a calmness will erase the worry or anxiety.

A third first aid technique to help work through a general fear state is to lie down and breathe deeply and rapidly. You can do this any time a fear feeling comes up. The deeper and faster the breathing, the better. If your legs or arms start to tingle or get numb, take slower and shallower breaths. When finished, breathe normally a couple of minutes before standing up.

Besides general states of worry and fear, you also need to come to grips with situations, circumstances, or conditions that scare you. These can sever your tie to money without your even knowing they exist. These could deal with business deals that went bad, or with a

137

near death experience from an accident, or the trauma of a divorce.

These are the types of fears you need to identify. These are feelings of fear that are associated with some set of circumstances. It is that set of circumstances you need to discover and address, but if you wrote down all the circumstances you thought gave you feelings of fear, you wouldn't make much progress. You would garner a list, but whether or not it would be accurate is open to conjecture. At the very least, lots would be left out.

Instead, you can uncover your fear-associations by adapting the techniques that have brought you this far. Not surprisingly, it is called PURGING FEAR-ASSOCIATIONS.

It begins with THE UNIVERSAL CONNECTION for about ten minutes. Then think, "Give me a set of circumstances that gives rise to a feeling of fear." When you think you understand a set of circumstances, verify them with your "Yes" and "No" signals. Make a list in your journal of all the fear-associations you receive. Continue this process for about ten minutes and repeat the entire exercise for several sessions. This is an ongoing process. Repeat this periodically.

The next step is to erase the association, which is simple, using our familiar invocation. This PURGING FEAR-ASSOCIATIONS begins with THE UNIVERSAL CONNECTION for twenty minutes. Then visualize the violet flame engulfing you and burning fear. Say to yourself or speak out the following or its equivalent:

"I invite all the forces of Almighty Nature, from every level of vibration, and from every realm, to destroy and eliminate from my life the effects of my inappropriate fears that interfere with my experience of prosperity, good health, loving relationships, and all other aspects of the good life, including but not limited to the circumstance of _____. All impulses I have sent out embedded with this fear are to be burned and neutralized. All subconscious thoughts that regenerate this fear are reprogrammed and substituted with life supporting subconscious thoughts."

Remember, by erasing, you only get rid of the debilitating nature of fear. You will not get rid of a positive concern that prompts you into some course of positive activity. You certainly want to retain that. It is only the fear-association without any basis that you erase.

FIRST AID FOR FEAR STATES

Technique One: Do whatever is comfortable to breathe fast and deep, such as running, walking, pushups, or sit-ups. Use common sense, and don't push your body beyond comfortable limits. Always follow the advice of your physician when exercising.

Technique Two: Sit comfortably and place your right thumb over your right nostril (or left if you're left handed). Breath in deeply, then out. Then move your middle finger over the opposite nostril, breath in deeply, then out. Repeat for several minutes.

Technique Three: Lie down and breathe with connected breaths (no space between the in and out breaths) that are deep and fast. If your legs, arms, or face feel numb or tingle, take slower and shallower breaths. When finished, breathe normally a couple of minutes before standing up.

PURGING FEAR ASSOCIATIONS

Begin with twenty minutes of THE UNIVERSAL CONNECTION.

Visualize the violet flame, whirling and flaming around your body.

Think or speak out the equivalent of these words:

"I invite all the forces of Almighty Nature, from every level of vibration, and from every realm, to destroy and eliminate from my life the effects of my inappropriate fears that interfere with my experience of prosperity, good health, loving relationships, and all other aspects of the good life, including but not limited to the circumstance of _____. All impulses I have sent out embedded with this fear are to be burned and neutralized. All subconscious thoughts that regenerate this fear are reprogrammed and substituted with life supporting subconscious thoughts."

Back off and feel the fear being turned away.

PART V   Wisdom for Living

Happiness depends upon ourselves.
Artistotle

CHAPTER TWENTY-THREE
Flowing

These invocations and practices allow us to flow efficiently through life. By determining our highest goals and establishing a plan of action, we can easily reach any goal. The key is to meditate twice daily, then to determine our highest goals and the steps to reach them using our connection to all-knowing intelligence.

The white water rafter has a goal and a plan of action. He doesn't head into the rapids blindly. He has a safe boat and a rudder, but he allows the natural flow of the water to take him to his goal.

It is just that simple for your goals as well. The almighty power of nature is your propellant. You decide your goals, you make the choices, and you delve into activity. It is the endless energy of creation that guides and carries you to fulfilling your goals.

Check your goals. After twenty minutes or so of THE UNIVERSAL CONNECTION and visualizing the violet flame, test your goals by asking and getting answers. "Is it in my highest and wisest interest to have _____ as my goal?" If not, find out why. After you have verified your goals, verify in the same way the first step toward that goal. There is no need to list all the steps. It is better to go one step at a time, verifying each as needed.

You don't blindly follow. It is not an aimless experience. We see people all the time who profess to be flowing, and we want nothing of what they're doing. They seem to lead lazy, shiftless lives without much purpose. They flounder from job to job. They eat from hand to mouth. That kind of flowing is like a boat without a rudder. It gets tossed around in the current, and anyone taking that ride is apt to get sick.

It is one thing to aimlessly submit to the pressures and forces around you and quite another thing to flow with nature with goals and with a plan of action. Don't abdicate your rightful throne. Don't lose your free-will. Instead, be empowered with all the forces of nature at your command. The king has all the resources of his kingdom, and he knows how to muster them. You are royalty, and now you know how to muster the resources of your kingdom.

The kind of flowing you're doing is powerful in part because of its efficiency. A skilled oarsman knows precisely the stroke needed for each maneuver. He would lose momentum and time if he had to experiment along the way. His skill assures him of victory. The oarsman wastes no motions, he loses no energy, and he gets maximum speed from his boat. So it can be for you. You can be skilled in all your actions. Quite spontaneously, you can go from step to step, wasting not a single breath, not a single step, not a single moment, and not a single movement.

Remember the race between the turtle and the hare? Each step the turtle made was a correct step in the right direction. He used his own resources for maximum efficiency. On the contrary, the rabbit wasted time, he ran all over the place, and he didn't focus on the goal. To any observer it would seem that the rabbit was doing so much more than the turtle. He was far more active. He exerted far more energy. Still, he lost.

It is all a matter of efficiency. Efficiency means skill in your action. It means you can accomplish more while doing less.

Flowing with nature is not copping out. Flowing with nature is knowing how to become efficient. You do this by first coming up with the perfect goals for yourself. These goals reflect your bag of talents, training, aptitude, skills, and resources. It just wouldn't make sense to take on a goal you were ill-prepared to achieve.

Next, you discover the steps that lead to fulfillment of the goal. You have to work; there's no room for laziness. You have choices; you can't abdicate responsibility. All the work you do and any decisions you make lead you to success. It is the most efficient system you could devise.

When you flow with such efficiency, you have the time and the energy to take on twice or three times the projects. What a dynamo you'll be. Everyone will wonder where you get the energy and time to accomplish so much. Feel free to share your secret with others. Your example is their greatest teacher.

When your flowing really gets going and you are very busy with all your projects, you may be tempted to postpone or forget THE UNIVERSAL CONNECTION. Don't. Make it a twice daily habit. It is the motor of your success. Each time you experience the deep relaxation that comes with the practice, you are recharging your batteries. They tend to fade after a few hours. The twice daily infusion is necessary to maintain peak performance.

Don't stop the habit just because you are busy. That is tragic. Time and energy is wasted, and you'll miss your mark. Whatever you lose by investing twenty minutes is made up many times with increased efficiency.

Flowing is quite dynamic, and it requires all that you have to give. This flowing uses every ounce of your talent and training, but it does not ever require something you can't do. The turtle used all he had, and he wasn't required to run like the rabbit to win. That is the beauty of flowing.

There is nothing that impedes your flow with nature more than anger. It is tantamount to the white water rafter dragging an anchor. It makes the boat difficult to steer. Forward progress is nearly impossible. To drag an anchor is downright dangerous. The boat might even capsize.

Anger is also downright dangerous. You know that. You've experienced it. Anger only makes matters worse because it cuts you off from the flow. You could neither learn your goals and your plans of action nor process them under the influence of anger.

In order to manage the flow, you must develop a way to manage anger. This does not mean you are never to feel angry. There are times when you must make a point. You must rise to meet an occasion. Being forceful, even temporarily angry, may be the only way to get a point across.

A quick fix to neutralize anger are the four words of THE LOVE CONNECTION: Love, Heart, Give, and Receive. From them make four sentences:

I give you my love;

I give you my heart;

I receive your love;

I receive your heart.

Then whenever you feel angry, look at or visualize the person or thing that perturbs you and think the four sentences until the anger subsides.

The anger goes. At least it smoothes over. Energy from those sentences is broadcast into the atmosphere. Although the person you're angry with won't hear the words, he or she responds to the loving energy. The edge is immediately cut and a semblance of reason returns.

Those words are also good for the slow festering kind of anger. Because our thoughts touch The Unified Field, they pierce time and space. Problems from the past can be healed with the sentences. Even rifts with people thousands of miles away or deceased can be cleared up. These words are truly precious, and they should become a regular part of your flow management.

You don't have to resolve the issue that made you angry before you think the four sentences. The issue and the feelings of anger are two separate things. Do resolve

147

the issue in time, but it can't be resolved while you're still angry.

These four sentences will help erase the feelings of anger so you can keep flowing. Once the angry feelings are gone, you can discover the first step toward a plan of action to unravel the conflict. Do resolve the problem. Otherwise you just might invite the anger to return.

Stay on top of all situations that might make you angry. When you come to grips with them early, your flow is hardly interrupted. Without dealing with them, they will create more problems and of course more anger.

Expert management of your life can be easy now. Practice "The Universal Connection" and "The Love Connection" regularly, and come to grips with anger. Discover your goals and the steps to fulfill them. The management of the flow is then automatic.

RELIEVING ANGER

Whenever you feel angry, visualize or see the person or thing that prompted the anger and think these four sentences:

I give you my love;

I give you my heart;

I receive your love;

I receive you heart.

These sentences can be thought for situations that happened recently or a long time ago. They work regardless of whether or not the person you're angry with is present, thousands of miles away, or even deceased.

Repeat the sentences as many times as needed to get rid of the feelings of anger.

WORKING WITH GOALS

Begin with twenty minutes with THE UNIVERSAL CONNECTION.

Then visualize the violet flame whirling around your whole body.

Think or speak out a specific question about whether a specific goal is in your "highest and wisest interest". Your head will nod up and down 3 times for a yes answer, and it will sway to either the right or left for a no answer. A "no" answer can also mean the question needs to be rephrased or that you should not know the answer at this time. Ask another question to clarify this "no" answer.

Establish in your own mind the first logical step toward that goal, and ask in the same manner if that step is in your highest and wisest interest.

As an alternative, you can ask for general information about goals and steps, such as asking what goals and steps would be in your highest and wisest interest.

CHAPTER TWENTY-FOUR
Ethics and Principles

There is only one ethical principle: do no harm. All other principles are a corollary. There are no other rules. Our only activities are to be that which are in the highest and wisest good for all. We can know that with the aid of a Negative Activity Signal, and we can use these invocations and practices to get answers concerning any ethical question.

All that there is in creation came about by stirring the Unified Field. Your thoughts reverberate onto a field of absolute silence where there appears to be nothing. They activate that silence into vibration, just as electrical impulses set a speaker into motion.

The Unified Field—The Creative Source—is stirred by the vibration of thought, just as it was stirred by the first impulses of our Creator's thought giving rise to our Universe. Once it gets started, the vibration grows larger and more complex, building upon itself. It continues to be shaped by your thought that activated it, but it is also influenced by all your other thoughts, by the thoughts in mass-consciousness, and by cosmic intelligence. In that way the world you experience comes about.

The more focused and the more powerful your thought is, accompanied by feelings and emotions, the faster and easier the results. Power comes from belief, feelings, determination, and being in the flow.

We manifest by attracting to us those vibrations in tune with our thoughts and feelings. If we intend to bring something into our life, the means to get it open up. Thought and feeling vibrations activate nature to spring desire into reality.

By being in touch with The Creative Source, the Unified Field, we are in touch with the most powerful center in Creation. Just by being in touch with it, we inherit and harness its power. Of course we can not be out of touch. The process has always been happening. That is the first law of nature.

The more refined aspects of nature are more powerful. When humankind split the atom, we witnessed a hint of the forces in the internal regions of creation. The Unified Field is the most refined, and we can't begin to imagine its magnitude. Its power is infinite. Everything that can be imagined can be manifested from there.

This power is yours without asking, but to experience what you want from it, you must tell the Unified Field what you want with your thoughts and feelings. When you are communicating correctly, you experience the feelings you want, and you are flowing with nature. However, if you abuse this power of nature to cause harm, your power is diminished or shut down. Suffering and lack will be your experience.

All the religions teach about the first humans. They flowed with nature in a beautiful place. All the forces of nature were there to serve them their rightful fruits. Somehow they abused the power, and they lost their flow with nature, leading to problems of all kinds.

The same is true with modern man. Until we realign ourselves with the fundamental energies of nature, life is a struggle. That is totally unnecessary. Humanity simply needs to return to the flow.

Returning to the flow is what you are doing with these invocations and practices. This has a profound significance in your life, and it influences all of humanity. Your awareness of your own power and of the flow of nature touches everyone. To some degree, you bring everyone closer to the flow each time you do THE UNIVERSAL CONNECTION because the orderliness of The Unified Field has such a great impact on mass-consciousness. Furthermore, the more other people are in the flow, the greater is a single influence. Eventually everyone shifts into the flow automatically without even realizing what happened.

A fundamental principle is that our power can not be misused without dire consequences. Your actions must always be in accordance with the highest good of the earth and all her inhabitants if you want a happy life. If you fall short, your power wanes. There is no probation or grace period. Whatever you do must be in accord with the laws of nature.

This isn't a burden. In fact, it takes more effort to lose the power than to keep it. It takes more effort to paddle up-stream than to float down-stream. Flowing with nature is the path of least resistance.

With these invocations and practices, you flow with nature, and you stay in the flow. All your goals you discovered are in the flow for the highest common good. Your guidance for each step toward your goal leads you only to supportive activity. Nevertheless, it behooves all of us to double check if there is any doubt.

153

Verifying The Highest Good is quite easy. After the twenty minutes of THE UNIVERSAL CONNECTION, ask, "Is such-and-such in the highest and wisest interest for the earth and her inhabitants?" If no, find out why. A simple revision might be all that is needed.

There is another technique to verify your actions are for the highest good. This is your NEGATIVE ACTION SIGNAL. Most people have already experienced this signal, though probably didn't realize what it is. With this signal you know before you do something if it goes against your best interest or if it is harmful to the planet or other people.

To discover Your Negative Action Signal, begin with twenty minutes of THE UNIVERSAL CONNECTION. Then think or say, "Give me a Negative Action Signal." You will notice some sensation that is uncomfortable. It probably won't be a movement, since you want to feel this signal in full activity.

You may not receive this signal on the first try, but don't fret over that. Eventually it will come, and it may come during some activity that is unwise for you to pursue. At that point you may recognize that this is familiar and has been with you all along.

The signal can come any time, and it always means to reexamine what you're about to do. It may mean you should abandon your idea, but it could also mean you only need to modify your thinking. The best way to find out is to ask after your twenty minutes of THE UNIVERSAL CONNECTION, using your "Yes" and "No" signals as an aid in getting answers.

Although the name of this chapter is "Ethics and Principles, there is only one principle: do no harm. All others are just a corollary of this one. If there is any question in your mind about a particular activity, you will know. The Negative Action Signal will be there. If it is not, you can ask and receive the answer by the practice of TAPPING KNOWLEDGE.

VERIFYING YOUR HIGHEST GOOD

Ten minutes of THE UNIVERSAL CONNECTION.

Ask, "Is (state activity) in the highest and wisest interest for the earth and all her inhabitants?" Use your "Yes" and "No" signals as an aid.

If the answer is no, find out why. A simple revision may be all that is necessary.

DISCOVERING YOUR
NEGATIVE ACTION SIGNAL

Ten minutes of THE UNIVERSAL CONNECTION.

Ask for a negative-action signal. You will notice an uncomfortable sensation that can be repeated easily in activity.

DISCOVERING YOUR
ETHICS AND PRINCIPLES

Ten minutes of THE UNIVERSAL CONNECTION.

Ask for the ethics and principles that are appropriate for you to keep in mind. Use your "Yes" and "No" signals to verify what you receive in your thoughts.

CHAPTER TWENTY-FIVE
Our Qualities

*We stem from and carry with us The Creative Source,
the Unified Field, from which all is created. As such, we
are creators, and our creations begin with our thoughts,
intentions, and feelings. Our lives immediately change
when we realize that and start living with the qualities
we own with the Creator: love, happiness, joy, bliss,
all knowing intelligence, perfection, peace, gentleness,
infinite energy, abundance, without judgment, and
timelessness.*

It is your natural condition to have perfect health,
abundance, and loving relationships. The first step in
living your natural condition is to know that. Knowing
is the key. You must know and accept the naturalness of
perfect health, abundance, and loving relationships for
that to be in your life. That is your very nature. You are
made one with all that exists. That means that all the
qualities of the creative energies and intelligence
underlying creation are also yours, including the power
to create.

Yes, we are all creators in the most basic, elementary
sense. We have the power to muster the energies of
creation to create our world, our experiences, and not as
just potential creators. We are already, in this moment,
creators. We don't need to evolve higher. We need to
learn nothing. We already have all the knowledge, all
the tools, and all the ingredients to create. We are an
expert at it. We have done it from day one, and we have

never stopped creating. The process is already one hundred percent efficient.

Creating begins with a thought accompanied by its feeling. That musters all the creative forces to manifest whether or not it is something you want.

That is why knowing who and what you are is of paramount importance. What you think and feel about yourself is your experience. Think you are frail, vulnerable, weak, or sickly, and you experience frailty, vulnerability, weakness, or sickness. Your ability to be a creator is so powerful, it can override, overshadow, and cover up your own perfect nature, and that is precisely what so many people do. Then they find it nearly impossible to grasp who and what they really are.

Oddly, the condition many people find themselves in is actually proof of their perfection. They are living proof that they do create what they believe, think, and feel. They believe and feel sickness is an inevitable condition, so it is inevitable. They believe and feel they are vulnerable to accidents, diseases, and stress, so they suffer. They believe and feel they have limited strengths, so they experience weakness. They believe and feel there isn't enough to support them, so they live in poverty. They don't believe and feel they deserve being loved, so they manifest toxic relationships.

It is a catch-22. The more they believe and feel they are weak, the weaker they become. And on it goes.

Their experience of what they think is so complete that they no longer see the cause-effect relationship. Weakness seems to be their nature. Disease and injuries appear to be random, arbitrary, and natural. They have dwelled so long on these mistakes that they think they are observing the natural scheme of life.

Well, we are all created from the COSMIC DNA. Call that intelligence, or life force, or nature, or whatever. The name is not important. The qualities of that COSMIC DNA, however, are important because they are the basis for what you are.

Within that COSMIC DNA lies the first stirrings of creation. That stirring is smaller than the most elementary particle. It is more powerful than the largest star exploding, yet more silent than nothingness. Within that COSMIC DNA lies the potential for all the multifarious forms in creation—all the life forms, the entire spectrum of energies, and the trillions of chemical compounds in an ever-expanding Universe.

Within each form resides the blueprint of the COSMIC DNA, like the sliver of the hologram film having the entire picture. Nothing is ever separated from COSMIC DNA. Within each form, whether a single atom or galaxy or whether a single cell or your Self, there resides the blueprint of the COSMIC DNA.

When you know this, you open yourself to the Truth of who and what you are. What you expect and believe changes. Instead of being weak and frail, you are strong. Instead of disease, you experience perfect health. The process is automatic. By simply knowing you are made in the image of the COSMIC DNA, you change your thoughts about your own qualities. That knowledge alone improves what you create, what you experience.

Before you can experience the perfect balanced life, you must firmly ingrain the Truth of who and what you

159

are into your consciousness. You do this by thinking qualities of the COSMIC DNA and accepting them as your own.

As you think each of the following qualities, be aware of the meaning that follows. Think of them at least once each day, at any time it is most natural. Perhaps you have a few moments after the alarm goes off in the morning. Maybe you can think of them as you commute to work. It is best to do this the same time each day so you can get a routine going. However, the important point is to think the qualities each and every day, regardless of when. The knowledge of "Your Qualities" is the backbone for all your other thoughts.

Think, "I am made in the image of the COSMIC DNA. Therefore I am LOVE." Love is a feeling of belonging. It is feeling unified with another being, any other creature, or any aspect of creation. You are connected to all parts of creation, and that connection is felt as love.

Think, "I am made in the image of the COSMIC DNA. Therefore I am LIGHT." Your own existence is proof of order and perfection. By opening yourself up to your own intelligence, you become a beacon of Truth so others can realize their own worth.

Think, "I am made in the image of the COSMIC DNA. Therefore I am HAPPINESS, JOY, AND BLISS." This is the state of mind you are created to experience. There is no need for a life of turmoil, fear, tension, or sadness. These come about when you forget your true nature. Think of a forest or a flower garden. Could those plants, streams, and animals be created from sadness? No. They exemplify joy and they exude bliss because that is the nature of the COSMIC DNA.

Think, "I am made in the image of the COSMIC DNA. Therefore I am ALL-KNOWING INTELLI-GENCE." The order of nature is undeniable. From the smallest atoms to the grandest galaxies, you live in a precise and orderly world. It is not random, yet it is infinitely complex. Clearly, that is intelligence, and you are of that intelligence. It permeates you, and you have total access to it. You can know anything you need to know.

Think, "I am made in the image of the COSMIC DNA. Therefore I am PRESENT FOR ALL TIME." You are more than your physical body whose main purpose is to lock you into this time and this planet. However, time and matter are not what they appear to be. Time is a function of relative speed, and matter is really just energy, and they are all made up of The Creative Source, the Unified Field. That is your true, ultimate body, and it is present everywhere for all time.

Think, "I am made in the image of the COSMIC DNA. Therefore I am PERFECTION." The COSMIC DNA does not create imperfections. That is why science can rely on prediction and orderliness. Whatever happens has a reason which stems from the perfect flow of energy. Anything that appears imperfect is simply evidence of incomplete knowledge, a misunderstanding.

Think, "I am made in the image of the COSMIC DNA. Therefore I am PEACE AND GENTLENESS." Underlying the dynamic activity around you is peace. When you feel it within, it is your foundation for strength. Gentleness is power. It is the anchor for all the forms and expressions of nature.

Think, "I am made in the image of the COSMIC DNA. Therefore I am INFINITE ENERGY." All that is

161

around you is energy. All the forms you see and hear are but expressions of energy. Even the entire cosmos is just a sliver of never-ending energy. You are that infinite energy. It is your dutiful servant.

Think, "I am made in the image of the COSMIC DNA. Therefore I am A CREATOR." You can stir the ethers of the simplest vibrations to create your own world of experiences. You can not have less than the COSMIC DNA. The building blocks to create any experience are yours for the asking. Just be certain you want what you ask for with every thought and feeling.

Think, "I am made in the image of the COSMIC DNA. Therefore I am ABUNDANCE." This naturally follows. Since you encompass a range from peace to infinite energy, you manifest your own world of abundance. The degree to which you do so depends on your own expectations, beliefs, and desires.

Think, "I am made in the image of the COSMIC DNA. Therefore I am WITHOUT JUDGMENT." People sometimes think they are being judged by their God. They even speak of a judgment day. Any judgment is simply the interplay of cause and effect. There is no intermediary step called judgment. You have the power to create anything. Just set up the cause, and the effect comes without judgment. Every person has that power, and it must be respected. Allow everyone else to create their own world. Don't judge them or their creations because you are not judged for your creations.

Think, "I am made in the image of the COSMIC DNA, therefore I am TIMELESS. Time is different throughout creation. At the basic foundation, where we ultimately reside, there is no time. We can play and create within time, while remaining outside of time. We have no beginning and no end.

The short explanations are only hints of the knowledge underlying these qualities. The important and only point is to think them each day. That lays a solid foundation in your thoughts to manifest the perfect life.

OUR QUALITIES

Think, "I am made in the image of the COSMIC DNA. Therefore I am LOVE."

Think, "I am made in the image of the COSMIC DNA. Therefore I am LIGHT."

Think, "I am made in the image of the COSMIC DNA. Therefore I am HAPPINESS, JOY, AND BLISS."

Think, "I am made in the image of the COSMIC DNA. Therefore I am ALL KNOWING INTELLIGENCE."

Think, "I am made in the image of the COSMIC DNA. Therefore I am PRESENT FOR ALL TIME."

Think, "I am made in the image of the COSMIC DNA. Therefore I am PEACE AND GENTLENESS."

Think, "I am made in the image of the COSMIC DNA. Therefore I am INFINITE ENERGY."

Think, "I am made in the image of the COSMIC DNA. Therefore I am A CREATOR."

Think, "I am made in the image of the COSMIC DNA. Therefore I am WITHOUT JUDGMENT.

Think, "I am made in the image of the COSMIC DNA. Therefore I am TIMELESS—functioning in time and outside of time."

CHAPTER TWENTY SIX
World Peace

*As we meditate and incorporate these invocations and
practices into our lives, our lives flow in tune with the
Unified Field and all the laws of nature. While
dynamic, we exude and feel peace. It takes a small
portion of humanity to be locked into such personal
peace to bring about a phase transition of peace for the
whole planet. That is the ultimate gift of this
knowledge.*

We manifest with our thoughts and feelings. A
turbulent mind with scattered, misdirected thoughts
and feelings bring us a personal world of chaos. If
everyone experiences a turbulent mind, the inevitable
result is a turbulent world. There is a definite connection
between peace of mind and world peace. They are two
sides of the same coin.

Both peace of mind and world peace affect material
abundance. A peaceful world cooperates to produce
infinite varieties of food and consumer products. An
embattled world requires sacrifice while the focus is to
produce bombs, guns, and tanks. On the personal side,
your experience clearly shows a rise in your own
productivity when you are at peace. Under stress, you
can't seem to pull it together.

Both peace of mind and world peace affect health.
Nothing destroys health more than a warring
environment. National resources are wasted on war

machinery instead of medicine. Furthermore, a healthy population looks upon the world differently than a stressed population.

If you are attracting only loving relationships, you let go of misplaced anger focused on outside peoples. When a whole nation does this, there is no energy for international conflict. Leaders view outsiders as friends, not threats.

The Unified Field is pure peace. At that level of creation, there is no activity, only potential. Nothing could be quieter, yet nothing is potentially more. In that silence, your thoughts stir "unmanifest" energy to give birth to a world of many and varied expressions.

When you do THE UNIVERSAL CONNECTION, your conscious mind dips into that silence before anything manifests. Like dipping a cloth into a die solution, your mind is saturated with the Unified Field in its most pure state, silence. That is ultimate peace, and you bring it back into your life when the session is over. You experience saturation of the Unified Field as peace of mind.

You don't become a zombie. The peace doesn't leave you lethargic. You aren't sleepy and lazy. This peace overlays dynamic activity. You feel confident and energetic.

The infusion of the Unified Field spurs intense activity accompanied with peacefulness. Such a great combination! The result is successful action. Your goals are quickly realized. Your wealth multiplies. Your influence is felt. Life becomes fun because you aren't

166

afraid. Besides, life is always fun when we're being productive without turmoil.

Being productive without turmoil: that is the gift of a peaceful mind.

There is nothing else to learn for this peace. It is there automatically. There is nothing to memorize. There are no new techniques to master. Just do THE UNIVERSAL CONNECTION and The Invocations. Get into the flow. Dip into The Unified Field. Become one with nature. That's all there is to it.

The "snakes" on the floor of a dark room are seen as mere ropes when a light is turned on. THE UNIVERSAL CONNECTION is turning on the light. With light you see reality. That is enlightenment. It is nothing more than being infused with the clarity that comes by dipping regularly into the Unified Field.

Regardless of whatever situation you're in, there is a solution. Always. Without exception. There is no problem that can arise in this world that is without solution. The real challenge is to correctly understand the problem. If you think the floor is full of snakes, you can't find a correct solution when the floor is only full of ropes. On the other hand, if they really are snakes, you can get the solution in the normal manner: set a goal and discover the steps one at a time to reach the goal. Every goal can be reached if there is clarity.

Remember, THE UNIVERSAL CONNECTION carries with it all the support needed to bring you material wealth, perfect health, loving relationships, and a terrific life experience. This is because peace is a prerequisite for flowing with wealth, health, love, and that terrific life. Without peace, the energy flow stops, and everything is thwarted. Everything you need in life is inherent in your connection to the Unified Field.

World peace is a reflection of collective peace of minds. If everyone on earth had peace of mind, war would be absurd. Whenever you take care of your own mind, you raise the possibilities of world peace to some degree. Clearly, the greatest single contribution you can make for world order is to locate and keep the peace of mind that is your birthright.

Furthermore, the principles governing mass-consciousness are also at work. Your state of mind influences everyone else. This is true because we are all connected; we share the Unified Field as a common denominator, and you make an impression in it. It is natural law, however, that you have a greater impact on mass-consciousness when you are at peace than when you're in turmoil. That is just the nature of orderliness. It is many times more powerful than disorderliness.

An example of the power of orderliness is the laser light. It is perfectly ordered light waves, and its beam can go to the moon and back with little loss. On the other hand, the scattered light of an ordinary bulb can be seen for only a few miles.

It is the same with your thoughts. Thoughts emanating from a peaceful, ordered mind inject that peace and order into mass-consciousness. Peace and order negate weak and scattered thoughts many times over. That is the key to world peace. It begins by simply bringing the Unified Field into your own life. It has tremendous effect because a little bit of order injected into mass-consciousness neutralizes tons of its disorder.

If we are ever going to obtain and maintain world peace, it must be by applying this natural law. This is understood by important groups around the globe. Many in their own ways are infusing order into mass-consciousness. You can do your share, which is significant.

You don't have to think world peace for this to happen. You don't even have to believe it. Just go after your own peace of mind by going after wealth, health, and love with THE UNIVERSAL CONNECTION, the invocations, and practices. World peace naturally follows.

PART V   Wisdom for Living

Science without religion is lame, religion without science is blind.

Albert Einstein

Part VI
Guiding Principles

PART III   Wisdom for Living

Most folks are about as happy as they make up their minds to be.

Abraham Lincoln

Chapter Twenty-Seven
Ten Directives

These simple instructions bring us in tune with our Selves and highest purposes. Meditate, have happy thoughts, think and feel what you want, enjoy diversity, give love, be giving, take responsibility, protect your physical body, and grow.

Here are some directives for living. These are only the essentials and are not meant to be complete.

It is important for you to understand that these directives will not make you evolve into a higher being. You are already there, and nothing can alter what and who you already are. That is ongoing and never ending.

These guidelines, however, will help you to experience a happier more fulfilled life because they will help you to manifest that.

First, meditate once or twice every day. "Meditate" means to relax and to allow your mind to connect to your source—The Creative Source, the Unified Field.

Second, only encourage thoughts that make you feel good. If other than happy thoughts arise, gently replace them. A happy thought can be as simple as feeling the breeze or smelling flowers.

Third, know what you want in life, then feel the emotion that comes with having it. Never think an affirmation if you feel the lack of what you're affirming. We manifest from our emotions, and the slightest feeling of lack will deliver more lack.

Fourth, marvel in the diversity of life. Enjoy interacting with all forms of nature. Know all forms come from the same source as you. We are ultimately one and the same.

Fifth, silently or verbally give love as often as the impulse arises. Thinking and sending love silently is every bit as powerful as saying it.

Sixth, be giving. Give your wealth to others. Give without expectation of anything in return. It need not be a recognized charity, but give to help another person, the planet, society, or the environment and all its creatures.

Seventh, make your environment a better place by not being wasteful, by leaving no footprints, and by healing the damage from others.

Eighth, take responsibility for your thoughts and actions. Realize you alone have created your situation. Realize you alone are creating your tomorrow—your "heaven" or "hell" whether here or in your life hereafter.

Ninth, love, respect, protect, and nourish your physical body. It is your vehicle for living here. It has needs and requirements. Be diligent in meeting those needs.

Tenth, grow. Grow by forgiving your mistakes. Grow more loving toward yourself and others. Grow your connection to your source, the Unified Field, The Creative Source. Grow your connection to wisdom. Grow toward a perfect life.

PART VI   Guiding Principles

Wheresoever you go, go with all your heart.

Confucius

CHAPTER TWENTY-EIGHT
Spirituality Is

Spirituality is a poem, a song, a dance. It expresses all we are, where we came from, where we are going, and why. It delivers our power and teaches us how to use it. It brings the reality of Oneness and expands our awareness to encompass all of creation. It is the supreme knowledge, all the laws of nature condensed.

Spirituality is conscious connection to the Self

Is our conscious source of Truth

Is our path for practical guidance

Spirituality is knowing love

Is giving our love

Is giving our hearts

Is receiving love

Is receiving hearts

PART VI   Guiding Principles

Spirituality is claiming The Creator's qualities

Is being happy

Is being joyful

Is being blissful

Is being light

Is being intelligence

Is being abundance

Spirituality is our Creator connection

Is being timeless

Is being everywhere for all time

Is being without judgment

Is being perfection

Is being infinite energy

Is being gentle

Spirituality is for friends

Is growing into oneness with each other

Is feeling the Unified Field

Is focusing on love

Spirituality is generating true forgiveness

Is knowing there is nothing to forgive

Is for giving and receiving love

Spirituality is social responsibility

Is correcting mass-consciousness

Is group commitment

Is slashing error beliefs

Spirituality is recognizing divinity in everyone

Is knowing we're made in The Creator's image

Is peace and respect for everybody

Is being without judgment

Spirituality is our relationship reality

Is our connection to our relationships

Is our source for relationships

Is our answer to challenges

Spirituality is our connection to our soul

Is our soul site

Is peace and well being

Spirituality is beauty

Is giving praise to our own beauty

Is praising everyone's beauty

Is bellowing out the beauty

Spirituality is loving our bodies

Is being grateful to our bodies

Is bonding with our bodies

Is filling our body's needs

Spirituality is manifesting our true desires

Is discovering our highest goals

Is thinking what we are to be

Is creating

Spirituality is spreading light

Is expounding Truth

Is radiating love

Spirituality is knowing who we are

Is knowing we have a divine purpose here

Is receiving cosmic energies

Is perceiving our holy tasks

Is accepting our roles

Spirituality is sexual acceptance

PART VI   Guiding Principles

Is the connection of sex with spirit

Is the dawning of enlightenment

Spirituality is being grateful for our mission

Is unifying again and again and again

Is dissipating negativism

Spirituality is hearing The Creator

Is chanting the vibration of the cosmos

Is calling home

Spirituality is being a Master of creation

Is being a Master with creation

Is being a Master in Creation

CPSIA information can be obtained at www.ICGtesting.com
Printed in the USA
LVOW091611070212

267552LV00006B/27/P